FINDING YOUR
YES YES YES

Living a Life That's Open to God's Invitations

CHRISTINE E. WAGONER

An imprint of InterVarsity Press
Downers Grove, Illinois

InterVarsity Press
P.O. Box 1400, Downers Grove, IL 60515-1426
ivpress.com
email@ivpress.com

InterVarsity Press® is the book-publishing division of InterVarsity Christian Fellowship/USA®, a movement
of students and faculty active on campus at hundreds of universities, colleges, and schools of nursing in the
United States of America, and a member movement of the International Fellowship of Evangelical
Students. For information about local and regional activities, visit intervarsity.org.

Unless otherwise indicated, all Scripture quotations are taken from the Holy Bible, New Living Translation,
copyright ©1996, 2004, 2007, 2013. Used by permission of Tyndale House Publishers, Inc., Carol Stream,
Illinois 60188. All rights reserved.

While any stories in this book are true, some names and identifying information may have been changed to
protect the privacy of individuals.

The publisher cannot verify the accuracy or functionality of website URLs used in this book beyond the date
of publication.

Cover design and image composite: Faceout Studio
Interior design: Daniel van Loon

ISBN 978-0-8308-4786-0 (print)
ISBN 978-0-8308-4787-7 (digital)

Printed in the United States of America ∞

Library of Congress Cataloging-in-Publication Data
A catalog record for this book is available from the Library of Congress.

P   23 22 21 20 19 18 17 16 15 14 13 12 11 10 9 8 7 6 5 4 3 2 1

Y   41 40 39 38 37 36 35 34 33 32 31 30 29 28 27 26 25 24 23 22 21

To Mom and Dad,
for giving me confidence to say yes

To JoAnne,
who pastored me through many yeses

To Kurt,
my love, for being a wonderful partner
in our yeses together

CONTENTS

．．．．．．．．．．．．．．．．．．．．．．．．．．．．．．

Part One

GETTING
TO YES

．．．．．．．．．．．．．．．．．．．．．．．．．．．．．．

Chapter One

. . . .

YES OFTEN STARTS
WITH NO

I would like you to consider leading your sorority Bible study."

"I don't think I'm the right choice."

"Would you consider going into full-time campus ministry?"

"Maybe in a decade or two."

"We are offering you the fifth grade teacher position."

"But I wanted to teach kindergarten."

"Have you thought about finishing that degree?"

"I'm too busy."

"You would be our first choice for divisional director."

"I wouldn't touch that job with a ten-foot pole."

"Would you write an article for our blog?"

"I'm not a writer."

Fear of failure. Lack of confidence. A limited vision of what God could do.

More often than not, I have initially answered no to what eventually turned out to be the most meaningful opportunities I've had.

This a mere sampling of the invitations God has given me in the course of my life and the ways in which I've initially responded.

My responses may seem rational. After all, people are busy, not everyone is gifted in the ways needed, and we certainly are allowed preferences. Sometimes I shake my head in amazement at how I went from "I'm not the right choice to lead the sorority Bible study" to landing in full-time ministry for the past twenty years. I followed a twisted path going from "I won't touch that job with ten-foot pole" to finding myself on an airplane bound for the divisional director interview in Chicago. And lately I've been laughing at my initial response of "I'm not a writer" . . . to writing this book!

We have the freedom to say no to invitations and opportunities; however, what if there's a yes buried in the no?

The first layers of reasoning for no may be the first steps in finding a yes. A journey that uncovers your desires, gifts, and calling. A process that brings confidence and clarity. An experience that grows your relationship with God and with others so deeply, you wonder how you didn't encounter this adventure before now.

Once a yes is finally found, it could bring healing and wholeness to someone's life. That yes might bring hope to a world in despair. Perhaps that small but mighty act of obedience to say yes, will bring honor and glory to God. And possibly God may want to use that buried yes to make a difference in a person's life or in this world . . . or maybe in you?

The first steps to yes often start with no.

MOVING FROM HERE TO THERE

What took me from the no to the yes? In short, the answer is Jesus. It's a very simple Sunday school answer, but it's the truthful one. Gravity pulls me toward comfort. Often my gut reaction is to stick with the first layers of reasoning to say no to all of these things. It's easier. It's safe. It takes less time and allows me to retain control over a portion of my life. Many of these opportunities placed me in unfamiliar situations and messed with my plans—plans I had for my time, my resources, and even my future.

Where does gravity pull you? Perhaps saying yes conjures up a level of anxiety as you think about the energy it will require and how it will disrupt your routine. Nervousness may bubble up around the thought of whom you may have to say yes with and work alongside. Maybe finding a yes is steeped in obligation. Guilt drives your yes, along with the familiar phrase, "I should say yes." Perhaps freedom to simply be open to either yes or no with no expectations would be a stretching invitation for you.

When faced with these risky invitations, fear can take over. But when I'm open to Jesus meddling in my life, then the journey begins.

This holy and sacred ground is where I turn my clenched fists into open palms. I start to release my grip on my life, trust Jesus with my fears in all their various forms, and believe that he has my highest and greatest good in mind. I choose to believe that he is doing something in my life that is purposeful and meaningful, and he wants me to join him in expanding his kingdom here on earth. I trust in the fact that Jesus knows me better than I know myself. If he is asking me to say yes to something, he must think I can do it, with his power moving through me. In following Jesus, he asks me to surrender to his plans and ultimately his love and leadership. This path from no to yes isn't easy, but it is transformative and can bring joy. It's not just for me; it's for you too.

The goal of this book is not to have you say yes to every opportunity that comes your way . . . although plenty of people would be happy for you to do this! The hope and prayer of this book is to create space for you to think and connect with God, yourself, and others, about being *open* to yes. Open to the path that could lead from no to yes. Open to the yes that invests in the kingdom of God—a path that leads to sharing God's love deeply and richly using your God-given strengths in a surprising way, and to knowing God's delight as you invest with your yes.

God could lead you on a path of discernment that points you in the direction of a solid no. It is possible that a no is the best choice. But too often we say no without considering our motivations or asking God for his thoughts on the matter. If we believe Isaiah 55:8-9, that God's ways are higher than our ways, and his thoughts are higher than our thoughts, then we must pause and consider the yes; consider what God might do, even if it seems crazy.

What would it look like to be open to saying yes?

HOW JESUS CALLS US TO YES

Jesus thought this concept of saying yes and investing in the kingdom was important enough that he included it in some of his final teachings to the disciples before his death. The disciples needed to understand what it would mean to live this life without Jesus physically present with them. Jesus had used many parables in the Gospels to describe what the kingdom of God *was*.

As he and the disciples traveled closer to Jerusalem, the place where Jesus would be crucified, he was revealing *how* to live in this newly described kingdom. Choosing to say yes and invest their God-given resources, time, and talents in the kingdom of God was a top priority for the disciples. They would be left to lead the mission of sharing the good news of Christ with the world. Jesus was leaving them in charge and would send the Holy Spirit to work in and through them.

He made it clear that the kingdom of God was to multiply beyond Jerusalem; it was to go to the ends of the earth. God wanted, and still wants, every people group in every corner of the world to know the transformative love of Christ. The disciples would be, as my pastor, Dave, says, "plan A" for leading this growth of the kingdom, including making more disciples and bringing love, justice, and healing to this broken world. The disciples had a big yes in front of them as they headed toward Jerusalem with Jesus in those last days, and so do we.

In Luke 19, Jesus tells the parable of the ten servants. In the story, a nobleman is about to go away to a distant empire to be crowned king. Before he leaves, he gives a pound of silver each to ten of his servants. The king tells the servants, "Invest this for me while I am gone." When the king returns, he discovers that two of the servants have made him a profit, but a third servant was fearful of the king and buried his silver in the ground. The king was thrilled with the two servants who invested their silver, and as a result, he gave them promotions to be governors of cities in his kingdom. In contrast, the king was furious with the third servant who chose to bury his silver. The king gave his buried silver to the first servant who had multiplied his investment tenfold.

For a long time, I understood this parable as great material for a financial stewardship sermon. I would hear this preached right before the congregation would be challenged to increase their monetary giving for the year or prayerfully consider their charitable contributions. As one who does fundraising for a portion of my job, I appreciate the application of investing our money into the kingdom of God, multiplying those resources as far as we can, and knowing the pleasure of God in the midst of it. This is not an incorrect application, but the vision is too narrow. This passage came alive to me when I began to really understand what Jesus meant by silver.

Silver was, and still is, a valuable commodity. The NIV translates this as "mina." One mina equaled three months of an average salary in the first century. It's reasonable to assume that Jesus primarily challenged the disciples and all who were hearing this parable to invest their money into the things of God and watch the kingdom, and their investment, multiply as a result. However, when we look at the texts surrounding this passage, we find people saying yes and no to investing different kinds of "silver" into the kingdom.

Earlier in Luke 19, Jesus interacts with Zacchaeus, a corrupt tax collector. Curious to know Jesus, Zacchaeus climbs into a sycamore tree to rise above the crowds and get a good look at him. Jesus sees Zacchaeus and states that he is coming to Zacchaeus's house for dinner. As the religious folks grumble about Jesus going to this sinful man's house, joy overwhelms Zacchaeus that Jesus would see him and want to be with him. Zacchaeus is so transformed by his time with Jesus that day, he gives half of his wealth to the poor and more than compensates those he cheated in taxes. Zacchaeus's "silver" is money *and* it's what happens in his heart. His "silver" is a vision to bring hope in the broken place of poverty by giving to the poor. His choice to say yes in using his "silver" is so deeply connected to his love and surrender to Christ that Jesus claims salvation for Zacchaeus. This yes changed the trajectory of Zacchaeus's present and eternal life.

In Luke 18 we see a different type of investment from the persistent widow. This is another parable Jesus told, of a widow who was seeking justice in a dispute with an enemy. The widow kept coming to a judge, asking for justice, and pleading for him to listen to her case. The judge finally relented and granted her request because she was driving him crazy with her persistence. This widow likely didn't have much in the way of wealth, but her "silver" was her ability to persevere and never give up. She used that endurance to influence the judge for justice.

Jesus uses this parable to teach us about persistence in our prayers to God, as God is a loving Father and will never tire of us.

I can't help but think of the good gift it would be to the kingdom of God if we had more people saying yes through the use of persistent and even stubborn prayers—saying yes to praying for justice for the marginalized, hope for the persecuted, and for eternal change in someone's soul. This, too, is "silver" in God's economy, which if invested, will surely multiply.

Then there's the story of saying no. In Luke 18, Jesus encounters a rich man who has followed the rules of God since he was young. The rich man asks Jesus what he should do to inherit eternal life. When Jesus tells him to sell his possessions and follow him, the man becomes sad. In the Mark 10 account, the man also walks away. Not only did Jesus ask him to invest his silver in the kingdom, he also tapped into a deeper heart issue. Would he trust that saying yes to Jesus would be worth it, that saying yes to investing his physical silver would bring incredible joy, fulfillment, and transformation to his life? That following Jesus would be more valuable than his wealth? It appears that at least in that moment, the rich man says no. He walks away.

And this is why yes often starts with no. I resonate with the rich man. It's hard to trust Jesus with the investment of my "silver" in whatever form that may be. One of the first steps toward trusting Jesus is remembering that the "silver" is actually his "silver" not mine. He is the one who gave it to me and wants me to grow the kingdom with it. It helps me trust Jesus when I remember that he not only gave me the "silver," but he gave me life. He created me and he knows me. He loves me too. This gives me courage to be open to yes, even if I want to say no.

A SURPRISING GIFT OF YES

A recent yes that started with no involved teaching this very parable at my church. In 2017, I received the gift of a discipleship sabbatical with the campus ministry I work with. As I planned for this sabbatical, I began to realize how tired I was, how over-committed I had become, and I was looking forward to some time to unplug. I also planned to enjoy some of the things I don't get to fully be present for in the midst of my everyday responsi-bilities. Cooking, extending hospitality to my friends and family, and reading topped the list.

A nagging thought kept coming back to me as I considered my list: teaching at our women's ministry at church. No. Way. I had taught several times in the past few years but had declined op-portunities recently due to work responsibilities. With this sab-batical approaching, the associate pastor asked if I might have interest in teaching again.

I didn't want to entertain this thought. Let me be clear, I love my church and I love women's ministry. I've been a small group leader for years and have even enjoyed the times I taught the whole group. I knew that teaching was part of the "silver" God had given me, as I had been affirmed in this by God and others for years. In my former life, I was a fifth grade teacher (another yes that started with no), but at first glance, this felt draining. It felt like I didn't have enough energy to spend thoughtful time preparing and planning for this undertaking. I felt exhausted and depleted. And honestly, I didn't want the extra pressure of performing that I put on myself for these types of things.

I knew how this would play out: I say yes, I try to prepare the teaching in the nooks and crannies of my other commit-ments, and then I wing a lot of the up-front speaking because I haven't had the space to practice the flow of the presentation. It would end up fine, but I'd be a nervous wreck leading up to the actual teaching.

No. This is not what God would have for me on a discipleship sabbatical, especially when I needed restoration of my soul. Or is it?

As I prayed, I wondered whether this was an invitation from God to remember my joy in teaching. Perhaps this was an opportunity to uncover the "silver" that had been hiding for several years? I used to teach much more at various college campuses and conferences, but my recent job responsibilities had required more time and a different set of skills. I no longer had the space to enjoy the study, preparation, and speaking that goes into teaching from Scripture. But as I prepared for sabbatical, God would be giving me space. A lot of space, actually.

No one begged me to teach, and I knew plenty of other women who would say yes. But I couldn't shake this nudging I sensed from the Lord. When I first started my relationship with Christ, I may have ignored these stirrings in my soul and stayed in my comfort zone. As I've grown with Jesus, I've learned to stop and pay attention. If I keep thinking of an opportunity or idea, I ask trusted others for their insight. I linger in the uncertainty. I ask God if there's something he is inviting me into. The invitation may go beyond an accomplished task; it may go straight to my soul and grow my heart.

What "silver" might be hiding out in your life?

To my surprise, the more I held the thought of teaching, the more it began to sound refreshing: prayerfully simmering over God's Word and being transformed by it, all while using the "silver" he had given me. And maybe God would have another layer of healing for me as I dealt with my performance anxieties. Maybe in this unhurried time, he would remind me of my identity in him and the peace that comes from this. It occurred to me that when we practice saying yes to God, we might not see the potential benefits until we take a step toward it.

So my no became a yes. One of my teaching assignments was the parable of the ten servants in Luke 19. Of course! God did all and even more than I expected in my risk of saying yes. He gave me energy to complete the task, I drew close to him in the process, and he blessed me with more freedom in my soul as I taught for and with him. So much freedom that I accepted another invitation to preach at my parents' church later that spring.

How could you create space in your life to pay attention to stirrings of the Spirit?

I'm grateful I didn't bury my "silver" this time. I'm thankful my no turned into a yes. The Lord continued to pursue me in using my "silver" this way, even if I wasn't very receptive at first. If I would have stuck with my no, several women in my small group may have stayed in their comfort zones instead of using their talents in new ways. If I held on to no, I would have missed out on the inspiration God gave me through this parable. Without this inspiration, there would have been no journey in writing a book. We miss out when we say no prematurely. When we do choose to say yes to invest in God's kingdom, he will not only grow the kingdom but will grow us as well.

The first steps to yes often start with no.

SPIRITUAL EXPERIMENT

Pray and ask God to remind you of any recent noes you've said. Spend time asking God if you might need to learn from or reconsider any of these noes. What might be gained from a no-turned-yes?

Chapter Two

. . . .

SHIFTING OUR PERSPECTIVE

The obstacle course in gym class was one of my favorite activities. I don't know what was so appealing to me. Perhaps it was the challenge to get to the finish line as fast as possible. Maybe it was the quest to conquer a variety of barriers. We jumped through tires, which required agility. Then we slithered through the plastic tunnel, calling for flexibility. Let's not forget about the climb up the rope to ring the bell! I had zero upper body strength and still don't. Nonetheless, it was exhilarating at the end of the course to feel like I maneuvered through all the different types of obstacles, or at least tried.

The obstacles prevalent in the journey to yes are not nearly as much fun as the course in gym class. These external and internal barriers hold us back from experiencing the fullness of God. There are many obstacles to yes, and I won't attempt to name them all in these next two chapters. We'll spend time unpacking a few. More may come to your mind as you spend time in reflection. It is worth listening to what bubbles up as you think about your own obstacles to yes.

Why do *we* bury our yes? What prevents *us* from saying yes, or at least makes us hesitate?

A limited perspective on our circumstances and our identity may create obstacles to yes. These limitations can be a byproduct of brokenness in our culture, or perhaps within our own souls. To be open to yes, we may need to shift our perspective on our circumstances, abilities, and even our core identity.

THE TIMING ISN'T RIGHT

The phone rang later than usual for a weeknight. It was Jill. She called to say that yet another dating relationship had ended up in shambles. We bemoaned together the hardships of dating in our twenties. That's when Jill had the brilliant idea that we should get a few of our single girlfriends together and travel to Europe. Seize the day! Enjoy the moment! Relish this freedom we have as singles (and maybe eat ramen noodles for the next six months to save for such a vacation)!

We rallied the troops and started planning for our European tour. Though I was excited about the trip, a piece of me was unsettled. I had always dreamed of a vacation to Europe. The romance of the cobbled streets, glistening ocean, and delectable foods . . . but with my husband. Mind you, there was no man in sight. Who knows when he could show up? Tomorrow? This month? Next year? If I made this trip, would I have buyer's remorse if he came on the scene any time soon? Then again, I didn't want to miss out on an amazing vacation and wait who knows how long for this mystery man to come into my life. I decided to pack my bags and board the plane with the ladies.

We landed in Europe and began our trek around the Mediterranean coastline. As we approached Venice, Italy, I knew I was going to love it. The smell of freshly baked lasagna wafted through the air. Brilliant colors of the ocean, boats, and architecture painted the landscape. And those gondolas . . . they were everywhere! After we ate too much gelato, fed the pigeons in St. Mark's Square, and tried on sundresses at quaint boutiques in town, we headed for the gondolas.

As we stood in line for our ride down the canal, I felt the familiar unsettled feeling—the lump in my throat and the ache in my heart. This isn't how I'd dreamed of taking a gondola ride in Italy. Roses, smitten couples, and an ambiance of romance surrounded us. Maybe we should pass on this and go back to trying on cute sundresses?

The source of my indecision was bigger than to ride or not to ride a gondola. It was a decision to say yes to opportunities now or say yes to time spent in the "waiting room" of life.

This would be a decision that I would make over and over again in the years ahead—a decision to embrace my current reality and say yes to invitations God gives me; to live life now and not for the future or to say no and wait until life circumstances are "better suited" for the yes.

What kind of waiting room do you find yourself in these days?

When we spend time in the waiting room, we wait for circumstances to change, and we decline invitations from the Lord. From our perspective, the current circumstances in our life don't seem ideal. We might believe it's impractical or not feasible. We should wait. Wait to graduate. Wait for marriage. Wait for finances to be in a "good place." Wait for kids to be born. Wait for kids to leave the house. Wait for retirement. If we're looking for them, we'll always find a long list of reasons to spend time in the waiting room.

Here's the dilemma: these things may or may not happen. In the meantime, there are blessings God wants to give and opportunities he asks us to consider. If we continue to sit in the waiting room because we fear risking our ideal plan, we may lose more than our plan. We may lose a front-row seat to his kingdom work or maybe a beautiful moment with friends in a Venetian gondola.

This isn't to say that a no is wrong or that waiting is a mistake. There may be legitimate reasons to wait. We will talk more about this in chapter six. It's the motive behind the waiting that matters. Is it a waiting that is surrendered to Jesus, or is it anchored in fear? Anchored in fear, I may anticipate disappointment with the detour and wonder if my needs will be met. Trusting Jesus with timing, I discern the opportunities and expect that he will abundantly provide for me in my circumstances and for my heart.

If fear is keeping us in the waiting room, sometimes we need to pause the no. We need to shift from our limited perspective to God's wider vision. This takes time and reflection on his character and abilities. In such times, I do well to remember that God is in the business of creative solutions. He can create a way forward, bring people together, and orchestrate circumstances in a way no one else can. God is able and willing to do this in our specific situations.

Perhaps a new job opportunity is being offered to you; however, you are in the midst of family planning and hoping a little one finds her way into your family soon. Remember: the same creative God who parted the Red Sea and provided a way forward for the Israelites is the same ingenious God who can provide childcare solutions when it seems impossible.

Maybe an opportunity to lead a Bible study on your dorm floor is in front of you, but your academic load is heavy, and you aren't sure you have the energy to lead. Remember: the God who provided the overwhelmed Elijah with a nap, snack, and ministry partner is the very God who can care for your needs as you step out in faith to lead others.

Or perhaps you find yourself on the riverbanks of Venice, deciding whether to sit in the waiting room or leap into the moment God has given you—afraid that if you say yes, the pain in your heart will be too much to bear because you lack what you think you need to enjoy the experience. Remember: the generous Jesus who turned gallons of water into wine is the same Jesus who can abundantly meet your heart's desires in miraculous ways, both now and in the future. He will not disgrace you and he will provide. And with that reminder, you can eagerly jump into the gondola, receive his goodness, and enjoy the ride.

I'M NOT COMPETENT

Growing up, my mom did most of the yardwork. This, combined with many years of renting houses and apartments, meant that I didn't have a lot of experience with outdoor power tools. As I began to shop for a gas-powered leaf blower, I had no idea there were so many options. I was determined to surprise my husband with this birthday gift, as he was slow to buy one for himself. We'd recently moved into a home that has many mature trees, and leaf removal was proving to be a full-time job. With the help of a knowledgeable salesperson, I chose the gift and eagerly gave it to my husband. He was thrilled with the leaf blower, though he did return it for one that packed a bit more power, and he wanted to show me the intricate inner workings of his new gift.

"I'm not mechanically inclined, honey. I don't know how to use things like this. I'm more of an indoor gal."

He was perplexed by my response. "I want you to try this. There will be plenty of times that you will need to use this when I'm not around. You can do it, I believe in you," he said with a smile, knowing I had no interest or desire to learn.

When would I actually need to use a leaf blower in an emergency?

I humored my charming husband and said, "I'll try, but I've never even mowed the lawn. My mom always mowed the lawn in my family. I tried once and did such a terrible job, she fired me from ever doing it again." This is also a good way to get out of such chores.

My husband carefully explained the fairly simple switches and knobs. But it was the cranking of the gas motor that intimidated me.

"Just pull it back with some gusto a couple of times."

I tried. Nothing happened. It puttered and stalled. Maybe it's broken?

He picked it up and instantly made the motor purr.

"See, I can't do it!" I exclaimed.

I married a stubborn man. He wouldn't let me resign myself to mechanical inadequacies. We practiced several more times, and there may have been a few frustrated phrases that left my mouth. And then something happened. All of a sudden, I started the leaf blower on my own. I blew leaves off the deck, our yard, the neighbor's yard, and felt an immense amount of accomplishment!

One could argue that was my husband's way of getting me to do more chores; however, he loves that leaf blower and would gladly use it every day of the week and twice on Sunday. In this small achievement, he helped me overcome my sense of inadequacy and lack of confidence. I had made my mind up that I wasn't good at something, I never had been, and someone else should do it. With a little bit of training, practice, and encouragement, I was empowered to use a new skill. And the deck has never looked so good.

The belief that we are inadequate can be another obstacle in our journey to yes. We don't believe we have the skill or knowledge to accomplish something. This, coupled with a low confidence level, tempts us to lead with a no instead of a yes.

A first step in overcoming this obstacle is to be honest about the inadequacy. Is it a real lack of knowledge and ability, or is it more of a feeling that you don't have what is needed?

It can be difficult to untangle the two, as they tend to feed off one another. Our confidence can be low because we really don't know how to do something, and we've either failed in the past or are fairly certain we would fail if we tried. On the other hand, we may possess the natural ability to accomplish the yes at hand, but we've not been encouraged to develop that talent, or we may have internal voices that tell us we can't. And yet another possibility is that our gaze is too firmly set on others who appear to be much more proficient in this area than we are, and the invitation should actually go to them and not us. Of course, our feeling of incompetence can be a mixture of everything mentioned and dozens more factors too.

Is your inadequacy a real lack of knowledge and ability, or is it the feeling that you don't have what is needed?

Admitting that we don't have the skills needed to achieve a task can be challenging. For some of us, the mere act of asking for help is a sign of weakness. If this is a struggle for you, it might reveal itself when someone gives you constructive feedback. Can you hear the ways you could improve, or are you defending yourself? That defensiveness may be a check engine light for our hearts. *When we defend, we attempt to protect. What is it that you need to protect?*

We might need to protect a lie about ourselves that we'd rather not attend to. Somewhere in the depths of our souls, many of us took in a message that our inadequacies have defined us as a person. It could look like the following:

- I am not adequate in a skill, so I am not adequate as a person.
- I don't trust my own judgment, so to be safe, we'd better let someone else do it.

- I can't do it perfectly, or at least "right," so I shouldn't even try.

These lies deserve time at the feet of Jesus so he can replace them with truth of who we are in him. God has plenty to say in Scripture on this matter. Here are just a few truths to whet your appetite:

- "Therefore, as God's chosen people, holy and dearly loved" (Colossians 3:12 NIV).

- "You are royal priests, a holy nation, God's very own possession. As a result, you can show others the goodness of God, for he called you out of the darkness into his wonderful light" (1 Peter 2:9).

- "You didn't choose me. I chose you. I appointed you to go and produce lasting fruit" (John 15:16).

- "For we are God's masterpiece. He has created us anew in Christ Jesus, so we can do the good things he planned for us long ago" (Ephesians 2:10).

- "See how very much our Father loves us, for he calls us his children, and that is what we are" (1 John 3:1).

When we begin to believe that we make God smile and his heart is for us, we can have security in Christ rather than in our competencies.

I am not great at memorizing Scripture, but the more I discipline myself to meditate upon these truths, the more secure I become in my true worth as a beloved child of God. My perspective shifts from my false view of who I am to a true view of who I am. When we begin to really believe in our hearts that we make God smile and his heart is for us, we can have security in Christ rather than in our competencies. And then we have freedom to learn and to try.

This obstacle of feeling inadequate is not unfamiliar to the human race. Thousands of years ago, Moses struggled with this obstacle and begged the Lord to send someone else to lead the people out of Egypt. Moses went back and forth with the Lord three times about why he should decline this invitation. Finally Moses pulled the competency card with God, as he thought this would surely convince God to reconsider his ask.

> But Moses pleaded with the LORD, "O Lord, I'm not very good with words. I never have been, and I'm not now, even though you have spoken to me. I get tongue-tied, and my words get tangled."
>
> Then the LORD asked Moses, "Who makes a person's mouth? Who decides whether people speak or do not speak, hear or do not hear, see or do not see? Is it not I, the LORD? Now go! I will be with you as you speak, and I will instruct you in what to say."
>
> But Moses again pleaded, "Lord, please! Send anyone else." (Exodus 4:10-13)

Moses was right in saying he wasn't eloquent. There is reason to believe that he may have had a stutter or simply wasn't winsome in his speech. Moses seemed to forget the other strengths God had given him (thoughtfulness, discernment, and advocacy to name a few), his unique cultural and ethnic journey (born Hebrew and raised Egyptian), and his ability to hear from the Lord (he answered "Here I am!" as soon as the Lord called his name).

The voice of inadequacy spoke louder to Moses than the voice of his strengths. Perhaps most important, Moses doubted that God would show up in the midst of his deficiencies. I empathize with Moses' anxiety and doubt. It can feel terrifying to trust God in these risky spaces, especially if our history with God is limited.

For those of us who have walked with Christ for years, we can point back to how he may have helped us in the past. Moses, however, did not have this history. God invited Moses to trust him in a tremendous way early on in their relationship. Understandably, Moses wanted out of this invitation and didn't hesitate to argue with God about it.

God's response to Moses reminds us that God is with us in the yes. He will provide what we lack, and he will ultimately be the one to accomplish the task, not us. We are invited to allow God to work through us, and we have the privilege of partnering with God to see something great happen. God didn't need Moses to lead over a million Israelites out of Egypt. He could have done it himself. He is God, after all. But God wanted to begin a relationship with Moses through this sacred yes. If Moses would say yes, even in the midst of his doubt and insecurity, he would be saying yes to developing a trust and intimacy with God that would later prove to be invaluable to Moses in his leadership and life.

As the story unfolds in Exodus 4, Moses said yes to God's invitation but only after God offered Moses' brother, Aaron, as help in speaking to the people. Moses was no doubt relieved to partner with his brother in this task. When we feel underconfident in our abilities, we can easily believe other people are better qualified. At this point, another shift in our perspective is needed. Consider this view: Yes, there are certainly more qualified people to do the task at hand. But God has not asked them to step into the task. He has invited you. For this moment in time, God has chosen you for this particular invitation and thinks you are the right person for the job. The results are in God's hands. It is our role to be faithful.

In Exodus 3, God called Moses in the burning bush, not Aaron. Aaron likely could have done it with God's help, and he apparently was a more gifted orator. But God called Moses.

Although God was angry with Moses because he argued so much about the invitation, he was merciful to meet Moses in his feeling of incompetence. God continued to lead Moses in whatever faith he could muster, and God revealed his glory one step at a time.

Moses eventually grew in confidence and got a front-row seat to God's liberation of his people. And Moses became known as a friend of God, trusting him with his life.

NOBODY LOOKS LIKE ME

Joe earned a degree in biomedical engineering from Duke University. He dabbled in cardiac research before he earned another degree, this time a master of arts. For twenty-five years, he worked for the same organization. Joe held various leadership positions during this time and is currently a vice president for the company. He receives frequent invitations to train and speak, both locally and nationally. And only in the last few years has Joe begun to call himself a leader.

It's perplexing to think a person with so many accomplishments and natural abilities could believe he was not a leader. One might quickly assume it's a case of insecurity and lack of confidence, akin to what we saw in Moses' life. But this wasn't the core issue for Joe, and it isn't for many people.

Joe's parents emigrated from Taiwan to the United States, and he was born in Cincinnati, Ohio. His family enjoyed involvement in their Chinese church. As Joe matured, the church noted his abilities and asked him to help lead. Joe exuded confidence in this context, and leading felt natural.

In the workplace, Joe experienced leadership differently. Joe remembered a particular situation that highlighted these feelings. "Earlier in my career I took the initiative to gather a group of peers to collaborate on some issues that are usually handled individually. When the group was affirmed for our approach, a colleague said, 'I just thought it would be a good idea,' giving the impression it was on her initiative. I didn't correct the impression. This colleague was generally regarded as the 'high potential leader' among us, and justifiably so. But I wonder if her ability to self-promote wasn't also part of the equation."

Joe felt different from his peers. Not only did Joe look different from others in leadership, he acted differently too. While they were White, he was Asian American. While they led independently and spoke their minds, in Joe's culture, leaders tended to lead collaboratively and reflected before they spoke. His colleagues took risks easily, while Joe's culture taught him to be more cautious.

Joe's cultural differences in his workplace weren't fully understood by his colleagues or even by Joe. Joe reflected, "I would defer to others, especially older peers, while many 'rising leaders' would confidently push their own ideas, even among older coworkers. I would attribute credit to others, even when I played a key role, while others would take credit for themselves. While colleagues took a conflict head-on, I would often find a slower and more indirect way of influencing the situation." Early in his career, these interactions contributed to him concluding that he was not a leader. With these underlying assumptions in place, Joe's journey to yes was challenged and even blocked at times.

Experts call these underlying assumptions unconscious or hidden biases. Hidden biases are "automatic mental reactions to members of particular race, gender, ethnic, and other groups." They

> can occur outside of our awareness and . . . can produce
> judgments that cause unintended disadvantages for others.
> In other words, hidden biases can influence our behavior

toward members of social groups, but we remain oblivious to their influence.

Everyone holds hidden biases, and they are far more prevalent than conscious prejudice. Often hidden biases are incompatible with one's conscious values. We don't realize the implicit messages we are taking in from our culture and social contexts that feed these biases. We then develop what become blind spots as we think about opportunities God may be giving us or other people.

From our limited perspective, we form obstacles to saying yes to God's invitations for ourselves and hinder other people's invitations too. The more we uncover these biases, the more we become free to imagine how others and we might step into new and unexpected roles.

I am a White woman who loves people, parties, and fashion. I am a good cheerleader, although that was not my team in high school. Marching band was more my gig. Leadership and influence have been part of my DNA too. I enjoy moving people toward a goal and developing their leadership along the way. However, I did not see myself as a "real leader." Though I found myself in leadership roles, it took me a long time to see myself as a leader. In my mind, a "real leader" had positional, organizational, and spiritual authority. And I saw most of these "real leaders" as White men with strategic strengths and powerful upfront presence. My leadership lane seemed to be caring for people, organizing social events, and facilitating learning in smaller groups. I don't have a commanding presence, I'm not a man, and strategy is not my forte. Without my knowledge, an unconscious bias slowly and firmly crept into my soul.

Circumstances and people reinforced this bias over the years. I remember one time in particular, when I spoke at a training event for college students. I taught from Scripture and casted vision for ministry on campus. I deliberately prepared and worked hard to contextualize the message for the variety of students present.

After I spoke, a young man approached me and said, "I have to admit, when you got up to speak, I rolled my eyes and thought, *Oh great. A blonde sorority girl. I'm not going to learn much today.* But you really surprised me and I learned a lot."

Needless to say, he had a blind spot for women, perhaps particularly blonde women who could preach the Word with conviction and application. I responded by brushing it off and accepted this backhanded compliment. I, too, was unconsciously buying into this blind spot. A narrative still floated around in my heart that said, "You aren't meant to do this kind of leading."

When God eventually opened a door that led me to a wider lane of leadership, I was very hesitant to say yes. Staying in my lane seemed to be a safer option. I supported and loved people well but didn't feel like I should be the one in charge. God used my dad to help uncover blind spots I had in my own leadership. My dad is a White man, with many of the "real leader" stereotypes I compared myself to. He continued to tell me that my strength in loving people would be one of my greatest assets in leading teams. My dad helped me rewrite a job description to better suit the goals I felt God calling me toward. He helped me learn how to "manage up" to my supervisors when I felt intimidated to voice my opinion. If it weren't for his support, I would have held back and gone with the status quo. Because of his encouragement, I have experienced fulfilling new roles at work, and I have used strengths I didn't know existed.

I realize how fortunate I am to have a father who advocated for me. I know that my socio-economic position has given me privilege to uncover some of these biases faster than others. I also acknowledge that being part of White majority culture in the United States has afforded me fewer obstacles than many of my friends of color and those from different cultural backgrounds. As my eyes have been opened to unconscious bias toward myself, I have intentionally uncovered unconscious bias I have toward others.

It is impossible to have zero unconscious bias and be a breathing human. It doesn't make you a bad person to have blind spots. However, it is part of our discipleship journey to acknowledge them, to lament, to ask for forgiveness, and to repent. As we create new patterns of thinking, we become savvy in our cultural intelligence and learn to love people different from us. We then become those who can advocate and dream for all people to say yes to many different kinds of opportunities.

It is part of our discipleship journey to acknowledge biases, to lament, to ask for forgiveness, and to repent.

Jesus uncovered biases all the time for people. He gave dignity to the Samaritan woman in John 4 by asking her for a cup of water. It was unheard of for a Jewish man to be in proximity to a woman, much less talk to her. Even more outrageous was that Jesus was talking to a Samaritan, from a people considered impure outcasts by the Jews. Jesus broke all the rules by looking her in the eyes, having a conversation, and asking her for help.

Through their interaction, we find out that she didn't have a great reputation in town due to her five broken marriages. This fact did not deter Jesus. It is worthy to note that this woman tends to be seen in a bad light due to her failed marriages. However, in ancient culture, a man needed little reason to divorce a woman. He could divorce with little repercussion and move on, but the woman would be left destitute, as marriage was her only livelihood in the society. Not only did the Samaritan woman have a broken heart, she may very well have had no money and no credibility. Jesus saw her situation and the injustice. He saw her dehydrated heart, and he gave a thirst-quenching, redemptive love that could only come from him. The woman was so amazed by this interaction and her own transformation, she couldn't help herself and ran straight back to her village to tell everyone about this Jesus . . . this Messiah . . . who had finally come.

Many people in the village came to faith as a result of her testimony and her introducing them to Jesus. Classic Jesus: he empowered a Samaritan woman to be one of the first evangelists in the Gospels. He saw her when the culture didn't. He uncovered the enormous blind spots, which were really prejudice fueled by hatred, and revealed the true talent and spirit of this woman.

Jesus stepped into the systems and structures of the day that said, "No, you can't be used by God," and turned the tables upside down. He empowered all people to use the talents God had given them. Jesus knew that we would need diversity of strengths and backgrounds in order to bring the good news of the gospel to so many different types of people. *It takes all of our yeses to heal this broken world.* May we hold courage for ourselves and each other as we journey to yes.

SPIRITUAL EXPERIMENTS

1. Make time to have a conversation with a trusted friend or mentor. Ask for honest feedback/observations about your gifts and the obstacles that may get in your way to use them. Listen and prayerfully consider the feedback.

2. Learning from people different from you is one step toward uncovering unconscious biases you may hold. Choose a book to read from an author of a different ethnicity than your own. Pay attention to what you may assume and new things you may learn.

Chapter Three

. . . .

DISCOVERING INTERNAL RESISTANCE

I *can't believe I'm considering this.*

This phrase continued to run through my head as I settled into my flight home from North Carolina. A regional director for the campus ministry I work with began recruiting me a few months prior to be the director of fraternity and sorority ministry in the Carolinas and Virginia. At the time, I led this type of ministry at Purdue University and thoroughly enjoyed it. However, this invitation intrigued me enough to book a flight and see what this opportunity could look like. As I flew back to my home in Indiana, I had a lot to consider.

It could be an adventure. I would start all over.

I'd lived in the Midwest my whole life. As a thirty-two-year-old single woman, I had the freedom to explore options and make a change if I desired it. This location did reach the top of my places-to-live list. I daydreamed of living in North Carolina. Who wouldn't love the temperate climate, mountains, beaches, and Southern hospitality? I'd always felt a bit misplaced in Indiana.

I had to be honest about the challenges of relocating too. I had developed a deep and wide network of friends in the Midwest, and my parents still lived in Indiana. I knew no one in the Carolinas.

God could really use you in the Carolinas.

This thought ran deep in my heart. After all, I am a missionary committed to going to places that need the gospel. The need was great in this region. These staff and students were without a leader, and if they had one, the ministries could flourish in a matter of a few years. Countless students could come to know the Lord, more staff could be recruited, and ministry would likely expand. On the other hand, before I left on this trip, the Midwest region did offer me a job position that would allow me to stay in Indiana. I would be the associate director for fraternity and sorority ministry in Indiana, Illinois, and Wisconsin, and I could create a new training program for our younger staff. I really enjoyed working with this Midwest team, and the new position would draw on my strengths in teaching and training.

If it's challenging, it's probably the godly thing to do.

As I considered these opportunities, I realized my high comfort level in the Midwest, both professionally and personally. The Carolina job would stretch me as a leader, and I would be called out of my comfort zone as I moved across the country for Jesus. And the need seemed more urgent there. The more I reflected on these options, it seemed like the short path to finding yes had me headed to the Carolinas.

CHOOSING JOY

Except there seemed to be a dull ache in my heart. When I disciplined myself to be still and listen to my soul, I felt sadness. I began to grieve leaving my friends and family. The lure of the mountains and beautiful beaches didn't seem to make up for missing loved ones. Although my grief seemed a small price to pay as I fulfilled the needs of God's kingdom, it seemed right, and even holy, to push through these feelings and keep my eye on the mission.

I didn't need to decide for several months, which gave me time to process with Marilyn. Marilyn was my spiritual director, who helped me navigate what God was doing in my life. I highly recommend such people. A spiritual director objectively and prayerfully listens to situations in your life and asks thoughtful questions. These questions help to uncover patterns that the Holy Spirit may be allowing in your life to reveal more of who God is or even invitations into knowing him more. Spiritual directors often offer spiritual practices to help us press into these opportunities with God too, which is exactly what Marilyn did for me.

She asked me to do the spiritual discipline of the daily examen for a month. This is an ancient discernment practice developed by Saint Ignatius of Loyola. I would take no longer than five minutes at the end of each day to reflect on what brought me joy and what was draining energy from my life. Another way to frame it is to ask what drew me closer to God, and when did I feel further away from God that day. Marilyn wanted me to keep record of this for thirty days and see if there were any patterns that developed.

At the end of the month, I was not surprised at the results. I told Marilyn I saw a pattern of relationships. I felt close to God when I was investing in relationships, creating new relationships, praying for people, loving on people, or just being with people. I love people.

Marilyn then asked the question, "How does this inform your decision to move to North Carolina or take the position in the Midwest?"

I looked at her with a blank stare. I began to cry and said, "It will be hard to leave my people. I'm a single woman and rely on my friends and family for community. They make me very happy. But there is a need I can fulfill in the Carolinas, and perhaps I just need to trust God to provide new relationships. Maybe I need to be stretched in this area. God can take care of me in the loneliness for the first few years."

And in a way that only Marilyn could do, in a very soft voice with knowing eyes, she said, "You've just told me a lot about how you think God works."

Silence.

As I sat in the quiet of the room with Marilyn, I couldn't understand what she was saying. She may as well have spoken Greek. Observing my inability to connect the dots and how important it was for me to get this, she stepped in. The next phrase Marilyn said would stick with me for the rest of my life.

"You believe that God is more interested in what you can do for him rather than caring for your heart."

This was one of those holy ground moments. This statement went beyond a job decision. This narrative of God shaped my whole life. It was the reason I put emphasis on my achievements and found my identity in my success.

It was also the narrative that made me angsty with God. I had given my life to serving him, and at the age of thirty-two, I had no prospect of marriage or children, which I desperately wanted. He kept blessing my ministry and leadership, but my heart seemed to be left out in the cold, and I wasn't sure he noticed or even cared.

Finding this yes was leading me into deep waters. I didn't expect to tap into all of this. When we are open to yes, God not only deals with the opportunity at hand but often our whole lives as well.

Marilyn sat peacefully in her chair, knowing she had rocked my inner world. She embodied compassion and tenderness as she handed me the box of tissues to wipe my tears. She didn't rescue me from this moment, as she knew I needed to work this out with the Lord on my own. She did give me a question to ask God in the next month before I would see her again. I prayed this question: God, do you care about my desires?

I spent the next month sitting in silence with God, asking him this question. I needed to get still enough to hear that quiet whisper of God. This is a form of listening prayer that can end up in a conversation with God. In the listening, I remembered Scriptures that point to his love for me and that he is a good Father. I was reminded of how much he adores me before I do anything for him. I recalled images of my own loving parents and how they love to see me happy. In my imagination, I saw a picture of a loving Father God who wanted to give good gifts to me. And I recounted the ways the Lord had worked through me to help people grow and give him glory. Could God honor the desires of my heart and the good works he has for me, all in one yes?

What do you believe about God's desire to see you experience joy?

In this particular season, God wasn't asking me to do the hard thing and leave my relationships. He wired me for relationship. God knew the joy my heart felt with depth of friendships. The Lord understood that as a single woman with my personality, these connections became all the more important to me. My friends were like family to me. I believe God offered me a choice, and I shouldn't assume that the most difficult path was the only path. I agonized over this choice at the start of my process, but it became easier the more I prayed and listened to God. I said yes to stay in the Midwest and was unapologetic about it.

Ironically, several years later, my supervisor decided to leave our organization and attend seminary. I became the primary leader of the ministry in the Midwest. As for the position in the Carolinas and Virginia, they received a wonderful couple (from the Midwest) who led and grew the ministry there.

God often places desires in our heart to serve as signposts guiding us to the yes he wants us to receive.

God often places desires in our heart to serve as signposts guiding us to the yes he wants us to receive. Psalm 37:4-6 says,

> Take delight in the LORD,
>   and he will give you your heart's desires.
> Commit everything you do to the LORD.
>   Trust him, and he will help you.
> He will make your innocence radiate like the dawn,
>   and the justice of your cause will shine like the
>   noonday sun.

When we seek after him and align our lives to his ways, our desires begin to align with his purposes. The things that actually bring us joy could be what he uses to bring healing to our world. To disregard these signposts is not only ignoring our own heart, it's shrugging off the intentionality of God who carefully placed those desires within us.

The path to yes is not always the hardest option. It could even bring you joy.

TOO BUSY

Perhaps saying yes isn't a struggle for you. In fact, you love to say yes. Maybe you've said yes so often that now you feel as if you are in the circus. Remember the clown at the circus that juggled three balls and then kept adding to the number? We waited in anticipation to see if the clown could keep all those balls rotating in the air. Saying yes to many things can lead to that frantic feeling of trying to keep all the balls in the air, paying close attention that nothing gets dropped. The world record for most balls juggled is eleven. My coordination limits me to two.

When we juggle too many yeses, a calendar with no margin can be the result. To say yes to one more thing is challenging. This becomes a problem when the next invitation to say yes could be the *better* yes—an opportunity that will give us more fulfillment, teach us more about God, and make a greater impact in our lives. Being open to the better yes is difficult when we don't have space to consider it.

Why are we so busy? What drives us to fill our schedules to the brim? Perhaps we will miss out on a better choice?

I am reminded of the story of Mary and Martha in Luke 10:38-42. Jesus was teaching in town, and Martha wanted to open her home to Jesus and his disciples. It was an honor to have Jesus come to their home. Martha leveraged her hospitality gifts for this visit with Jesus and his disciples. I can imagine her pulling together food from the fridge, getting beverages on the table, cleaning the house, and if she was anything like me, she might be kicking herself that she hadn't made it to the market earlier that week to get those favorite snacks. Martha wanted to make sure all was ready for these notable guests. She was very busy getting important tasks done.

And where was her sister, Mary? She wasn't in the kitchen helping Martha. Instead, Mary sat at the feet of Jesus. Mary wanted to be with Jesus, to learn from him, to be in his presence.

Martha was frustrated with her sister's choice and let Jesus know about it. "Lord, don't you care that my sister has left me to do the work by myself? Tell her to help me!"

Jesus responded, "Martha, Martha, . . . you are worried and upset about many things, but few things are needed—or indeed only one. Mary has chosen what is better, and it will not be taken away from her" (Luke 10:40-42 NIV).

This familiar text tends to make me feel guilty if I don't drop everything to have a spiritual moment with Jesus. And Martha manages to get a bad rap in this story. She was too busy with cooking and cleaning; therefore she didn't say yes to spend time with Jesus. Mary is usually highlighted as the one who had her priorities straight and let the to-do list go to say yes to Jesus. And for good reason, as Jesus does highlight this choice as better, but it wasn't that easy for Martha . . . or Mary.

Cultural expectation was one reason Martha occupied herself with these tasks. It was expected that the women in this time period be the keeper of the home. Guests would drop by for a meal, and the women would be expected to have a spread of food and drink ready for their guests. It was also a cultural expectation for women to be in the kitchen while the men were in the living room talking, or in this case, listening to Jesus. Women had no place in conversations with men, especially when it related to learning theology. It's easy to see why Martha was busy with things that were culturally acceptable and expected.

Martha's busyness wasn't entirely bad. Jesus said that Mary had chosen what was "better." This implies that what Martha did was not wrong, and it was actually good. The Middle Eastern culture placed a high value on hospitality, and still does. Generosity and inclusion of all guests, even strangers, is not only a Middle Eastern priority, it is a value Jesus taught.

Earlier in Luke 10, Jesus sent out seventy-two disciples to spread the news of the coming kingdom of God and heal in his name. Jesus instructed them to find people of peace and "Don't move around from home to home. Stay in one place, eating and drinking what they provide. Don't hesitate to accept hospitality, because those who work deserve their pay" (Luke 10:7). Hospitality was needed to help the news of Christ spread beyond Jerusalem.

Then, in Luke 10:25-37, Jesus discusses the importance of loving your neighbor as yourself. He illustrates this point with the parable of the Good Samaritan, who became the unlikely example of abundant provision and care for a stranger.

Perhaps Luke is highlighting the kingdom value of hospitality and Martha's desire to embody it. She served Jesus and the disciples. She desired to be near Jesus and invited him to her home. She wanted to provide an opportunity for others to experience Jesus, too, and went to work in the kitchen to ensure they had what they needed to enjoy the day. Serving likely was something Martha did well, and it is a kingdom value. These are good things to say yes to.

As Martha prepared to host Jesus and his friends, she may have said yes to so many good tasks that she didn't have the bandwidth to consider another yes that day. There was a better yes—to spend time with Jesus and the disciples. Perhaps Martha couldn't consider this option because she held tightly to the expectations of others and her desire to serve everyone well.

It may also have been easier for Martha to choose to stay busy in the kitchen. If she slowed down from serving and sat with Jesus, what might have emerged from her heart? Would Jesus have rebuked her for being upset with Mary? What might Jesus ask of her? Yes, being busy in the kitchen seemed like the way to go.

Meanwhile, Mary stepped outside the box. In fact, Mary created a brand-new box. It was unheard of for women to do what Mary did. She went against cultural norms, took a risk, and learned from Jesus, alongside the men. While Judaism did not forbid women from learning the Torah, they certainly weren't meant to learn with men. Women were a rejected group in this time period, and it was rare to find a rabbi who would sink to the level of teaching women.

This was a bold move for Mary, and I wonder how she had the courage to do this. I'm curious about how the disciples reacted; Mary rocked the ship and didn't seem to care. Was she able to slow down enough to weigh out her options that day? Maybe Mary had the time that day to sense the power of Jesus drawing her toward him as well as his desire to spend time with all people. Jesus didn't filter people out due to their race, gender, or social status. Maybe that was why Mary thought it was safe to say no to the expected things and say yes to this unexpected opportunity.

I desire to be like Mary and can relate to Martha. Sometimes I stay busy in the kitchen saying yes to many good things because that's what I know, and people expect it of me. I can please a lot of people and get much accomplished. This can make me feel significant and loved all at the same time. These are not bad emotions, but when I derive more significance and love from people than from God, I know I'm headed down a path that will not satisfy. Not to mention that when I'm busy with all the good yeses, I don't have time to pay attention to my own soul or talk to God about any of the difficult emotions that may be beneath the surface of my heart. It's no wonder I can have a hard time finding space for a better yes.

I wonder what would have happened if Martha had given in to a better yes? Perhaps it would have been an opportunity for Martha to realize how hungry her soul was for Jesus' words. Maybe she would have felt freedom to let go of expectations and rest in the presence of Christ. In the big scheme of things, the hours Martha utilized were not large blocks of time but were meaningful. Not all better yeses are large time commitments. It could look like having time to say yes to walk with a neighbor you've been praying for. Maybe slowing down your pace means being available to sit in a doctor's office with a friend as she receives the test results she's been worried about. Perhaps margin in your calendar will allow you to pray for and be more present with colleagues in your office. If we've said yes to too many things, we often can't say yes to these small opportunities with a big impact.

What smaller, better yeses would you enjoy considering if you had time?

If you resonate with saying too many yeses for one reason or another, I commend this practice to you before you give your next yes: Sleep on it. Or at least wait a minute or two before you agree. Ask the Lord in a time of prayer what his thoughts are on the matter. Will you have margin to be present with others and with God if you say yes? And reflect on your motivation for saying yes. Are you looking to him or external factors for fulfillment in this yes?

Martha's yes to serving Jesus and the disciples was a good yes, but Jesus wanted her to consider a better yes that day. If she could have let go of some of those good other tasks, Jesus knew that Martha's heart would have benefited from time spent with him. She would have known how loved she was by the Lord and that she, too, had a place in the living room with Jesus.

FEAR OF FAILURE

I listened to the voicemail again. The message was an invitation to consider directing the Women's Daniel Project, a leadership cohort for women in my organization, which would prepare participants for senior leadership. This was a national program that would receive a lot of attention from colleagues. If done well, it would bless our organization with eighteen talented women leaders who were equipped with confidence, vision, and skill, and were ready to step into greater influence and leadership. This could help our leadership pipeline flow with new energy. We could see our ministry refreshed and ultimately more students coming to know the Lord.

When I received this invitation, my first response was no. I initially said that I was too busy. I was juggling too many balls in the air and couldn't imagine adding one more to the mix, especially a big beach ball like this cohort. Many people agreed with me, and it seemed logical and right to say no.

Several months passed, and I was invited again to consider this opportunity. The timeline for the project had been pushed back.

A knot formed in my gut.

This new timeline would work much better for me. I could figure out how to do this. On the other hand, I bet I could still play the busy card, if I wanted to.

Why was this knot in my gut?

Probably the stress of being too busy and not being able to take this on. Why stress myself out over this? I should say no, again.

As I spent time discerning this invitation, I realized it wasn't my busyness that created this knot in my stomach. This knot served as another one of those check engine lights in my soul. It's interesting how God wired us so intricately that even our physical feelings may help us discern our choices. Once I slowed down from the hustle and channeled my "inner Mary," I discovered a deeper reason for my no. Busyness became my excuse to avoid this opportunity. I was scared. If I chose to do this, fear surrounded my heart because this national cohort had a very public stage in our organization. If this went sideways, everyone would know, and I would be the face of that failure.

Nothing kills taking a risk like the fear of failure.

I have built my life around avoiding failure, and I am very hesitant to take risks if I think there's a chance I won't do well. My motivation for avoiding failure boils down to averting embarrassment. I care too much about my image and what people think.

I have been helped by learning the Enneagram, an ancient assessment that identifies our core motivations in dealing with others, the world, and ourselves. It highlights how we are wired, both positively and negatively. My Enneagram number, Three, the performer, confirmed my value for productivity and my motivation to appear capable while doing it. There are some upsides to this: I get a lot done and I do it well. People are very pleased with my outcomes, and it evokes confidence on the teams I lead. The downside is, if I'm operating out of my own strength, I can be a bit of a train wreck internally.

I strive to make the tasks, the team, and the processes I lead go swimmingly well, because I want to avoid failure with everything I've got. The worst thing I could do is fail, because that would mean others might discover what I tend to believe at the core of my being: I'm inadequate. Which leads to the shameful thought: I'm not good.

The Enneagram gives paths to healing, and in God's ironic way, the path to redeeming my need to achieve is through failure. I must fail in order to know that God loves me at my core, no matter what kind of success or failure I experience. As I receive his love through Christ, I can peel off this heavy coat of shame. For me, this is a continual process of shedding layers of the coat. The more I take in God's grace, the more freedom I have to step out and try new things. I am worthy in him, no matter the outcome or what people think.

Fear of failure can take many shapes and sizes. Maybe you avoid failure because of your desire for perfection. Or perhaps a feeling of obligation drives you to not let others down or allow the task to fail. It's important to spend time understanding ourselves better, even the shadow sides of us, so we can identify places where we could be blocking a yes to God. We might be getting in our own way and not even know it, not to mention the ease and joy we can have to say yes without fear and shame hindering us.

I am a big fan of counseling. Through therapy, I have learned a lot about myself and these shadow sides. It is an investment of time and resources. My counselor, Trudy, encouraged me to look at life like a learning lab. This place on earth is where we get to learn. We get to practice different ways of living a life that honors Christ. Scripture tells us we are in a sanctification process, where we learn what it means to be more like Jesus and prepare ourselves to live in heaven with him one day.

We get lots of opportunities to practice the ways of Jesus as we interact with people and engage in the world. A step in finding a yes may be to say, "I'll try." When we step out and try, we release that fear of failure and receive the love of Christ. We can then start to love ourselves, even the unpolished, broken parts of us.

A step in finding a yes may be to say, "I'll try."

I'm grateful for God's abundant grace and perseverance with me as I learn to try new things and say yes. As I spent time in reflection, I realized I buried my "silver" with the first invitation to direct the Women's Daniel Project. Yes, I was busy, the timing wasn't great, and I had a decent amount of fear of failure. God must have known how transformative this yes would be for me, if I would only try. It ended up being one of the best experiences I've had in two decades of ministry. I suspect that's why he was gracious and gave me a second opportunity to say yes. Perhaps God also knew how much I needed to trust his love for me. I needed this yes to learn, once again, that whether I succeeded or failed, I would still be a beloved child of God.

SPIRITUAL EXPERIMENT

Practice the daily examen in the next week. Take no more than five minutes at the end of each day to reflect on when you felt near to God and when you felt distant from God. In a journal or electronic device, write your responses. At the end of the week, observe if there are patterns that indicate places of joy or places of angst. How could this help you be open to a yes God may have for you?

· ·

Chapter Four

STARTING SMALL

Christine, a friend who happens to share my name, arrived in Bangkok, Thailand, and felt the heat of the earth on her face. The city reminded her of other metropolitan cities she'd visited. Beautiful architecture gave shape to the buildings. The flowers bloomed in gorgeous colors and decorated the city. And the wealth of the city became apparent through one of the world's largest shopping malls located in a nearby suburb. But when Christine turned down a side street into the red-light district, the scene changed dramatically. Homeless people lined the sidewalks. Bars with names like "Lollipop" lined the streets. And then Christine faced the horrifying sight of thousands of girls being sold for sex, lifelessly dancing in the windows of those bars. She wondered if her heart could take this all summer.

Christine had followed a typical script for her life at nineteen years old. As a sophomore in college, she dedicated time to her studies and enjoyed hanging out with friends. She volunteered at her church and nurtured her faith in Jesus. Curiosity about the world filled Christine's soul. She desired to know more of God's movement in cultures other than her own. Christine said yes and served on the missions team at her church, alongside her father, who happened to lead the global efforts there.

It was 2008, and the issue of human trafficking and sexual exploitation became more visible in the United States. The global team at her church began researching organizations that confronted this broken place of injustice. As Christine did the research, her heart began to break. She started to think, *Is this really true? Are there women my mother's age, my age, and even younger, who are being sold for sex?*

Her mind could barely comprehend that this level of evil existed. As Christine learned more about the atrocities happening to young women caught in the grip of sex trafficking, she felt very unsettled. She became convinced that this was an area her church should help to heal. But how?

A ministry called the Beginnings Foundation in Bangkok, Thailand, led by a retired schoolteacher came to the attention of Christine and the missions team. After several months of research and prayer, Christine and one of her teammates said yes to the invitation to fly to Thailand for the summer. They wanted to learn more about this ministry and how the issue of sexual exploitation manifested itself in this corner of the world. Christine hoped that as she served this summer, God would use her to help rescue these girls from the bars where they were sold. Their whole lives could change if Christine could just get them out.

When Christine and her teammate arrived in Bangkok, they received a warm welcome from Bonita and the residents at Beginnings. Bonita had started this ministry in Bangkok after her husband's job relocated them to the city. They had moved from Washington, DC, and Bonita had planned to enjoy her retirement. She did not plan for the horrible poverty and injustice surrounding her and the hundreds of girls being sold for sex as a result. She couldn't just sit by and watch this happen. As Bonita interacted with some of the women in the red-light district, she understood more of their stories. In this culture, the oldest child provides income for impoverished families. The daughters have very little value in their society, but they can make money and bring honor to their family if they sell themselves for sex. And there are plenty of men eager to pay for their services. Bonita couldn't stand by and watch this happen. God invited her to say yes to loving these women and helping them find a new way of life.

As Christine learned from Bonita about the culture and ministry, horror and sadness surrounded her on the streets of the district. It was worse than she'd imagined. Thousands of women were sexually exploited. These perpetrators sold the women like pieces of meat every night. They stood on the nightclub bar with numbers hung around their necks, waiting to be chosen like items on a menu. As the women stood waiting to be purchased, their eyes were empty of emotion and total despair surrounded them. Christine felt physically sick to her stomach when she learned that customers would choose the number and pay a "bar fine" to have the right to that girl for the day and night. That fine was typically around twenty-four dollars.

These precious humans were women whose choices had been taken away for a variety of reasons. More powerful people had used coercion and intimidation as a means to sell them for sex. Many of these victims had no other option as they lacked the skills and education needed for a viable income. All of the women had been stripped of their dignity and self-worth by this evil, thriving industry. The system they lived under made it nearly impossible to survive in any other manner. The cycle trapped the women with no way out. It was heartbreaking. Christine realized she couldn't simply rescue these girls out of the bars. It was much more complicated.

Christine's heart continued to break as she ministered to women alongside Bonita and the Beginnings Foundation. Bonita and her team extended the compassion and love of Jesus to these women in emotional, spiritual, and practical ways. Many developed marketable skills through the help of Bonita's team. As a result, the women provided money for their families in new ways. They grew in confidence and self-worth as they developed their skills. Most importantly, Christine had a front-row seat in watching the abundant love of Christ flow through the Beginnings Foundation team and to these women. Hope glimmered from this dark place. Christine determined to get more resources and help this ministry reach even more girls. Again, the question, *But how?* lingered in the air.

When the summer came to an end, Christine flew back home ready to advocate for this ministry. She seared the images and stories into her mind in an effort to never forget these girls. She wondered how she could help raise the awareness of this issue on her college campus and around her community. She resolved to do something, even if it was a small step.

Christine's first step was to solidify the partnership between her church and the Beginnings Foundation. As Christine shared her stories from the summer, it was abundantly clear that God was working beautiful stories of redemption that they were eager to be a part of. Financial resources along with short-term mission trips were underway. Christine didn't limit her efforts to help the Beginnings Foundation to her church alone.

She resolved to do something, even if it was a small step.

Next, she looped her friends in on the possibilities of partnership too. Christine conveyed what she'd witnessed in the red-light district and shared the stories of the women she'd met.

Moved by Christine's vision, her friends desired to do something as well.

Another small step evolved in Christine's mind.

Numerous organizations sold T-shirts to promote and raise money for a cause. College students enjoyed sporting these T-shirts as well as supporting a charity. Why couldn't something similar happen to help support the work of Bonita and her team?

Using their connections and creativity, these college students began buying and selling T-shirts with "Freedom 4/24" as their logo. Christine couldn't shake the reality that halfway around the world, women were being sold for twenty-four dollars—such a trivial number. What if she and her friends could use that same amount—twenty-four dollars—and instead rally people to give that money toward bringing freedom through the support of the Beginnings Foundation?

The T-shirts were a hit beyond what anyone could have expected. Sales raised thousands of dollars to support the Beginnings Foundation. Their product raised awareness and concern, and Freedom 4/24 allowed people to contribute to the cause or be directly connected to support the work of Beginnings. As T-shirt sales continued to climb, so did Christine's understanding of the global issue of human trafficking and sexual exploitation. Though perhaps more conspicuous in other parts of the world, this was by no means an issue unique to one region. In reality, this was happening all around the globe and in her own city.

Eventually, Freedom 4/24 went beyond a logo on T-shirts and launched a local 5K to raise even more funds. This money aids the work of the Beginnings Foundation in Bangkok as well as other partnerships in Uganda, India, and around the United States.

Soon, word got out to other college students on other campuses. They, too, wanted to sell T-shirts and host races. Christine tried to keep up with what God was doing and often felt several steps behind. But God always brought along people to carry the mission forward. Before she knew it, Freedom 4/24 became much more than a simple T-shirt fundraiser.

Ten years later, Freedom 4/24 is an international nonprofit that has raised hundreds of thousands of dollars and transformed hundreds of women and their families, all to the glory of God.

Christine had to say yes to many small things before Freedom 4/24 became established. It's often in the small yeses that God grows our confidence and vision for what he has planned next. When Christine was a college sophomore, she wasn't thinking she would become the founder of an international nonprofit. She had no idea that a recovery house for sex-trafficked women in Uganda would be named after her. Christine reflected:

It's often in the small yeses that God grows our confidence and vision for what he has planned next.

The vision wasn't for it to be this big nonprofit organization. The vision was T-shirts. Why? Because T-shirts were easy. They were within my control. Honestly, they didn't require a ton of faith. But God loves to grow our faith. He loves to work through weakness, so that all the world can see is his power. Throughout the growth of Freedom 4/24, it was a constant yes to the Lord. I was just walking into what God gave me and catching up to his vision for it. Here's the thing I wrestled with: Where is the balance of operating within your giftings and getting pushed out of your comfort zone? I feel like God has gifted me to be in supportive roles far more than in leadership roles. I don't have any interest in being the person up front. I enjoy being behind the scenes and encouraging people.

This is precisely why it took her even more courage to say yes as God kept growing this movement into a successful nonprofit. Requests for Christine to participate in interviews or speak to huge crowds in the keynote role stretched her far beyond her level of comfort. This was not what she'd had in mind, but she wanted to keep giving God her yes.

In God's unique design, he fostered the growth and redemption of multiple people and places. God used the success of this nonprofit to bring healing to sex-trafficked women. Thousands of people moved from inaction to engagement in kingdom work. At the same time, God was growing and teaching Christine in her leadership and discipleship. She trusted him with her inadequacies, put faith in his ability to work through her, and learned to lean on him for peace when she felt anxious about where all of this was going.

As Freedom 4/24 grew, so did Christine. In the same way she trusted Jesus with the kingdom work he was doing in these sexually exploited women, she trusted him for the kingdom work in her own heart. While she wanted to be faithful to God's call, she also wanted to pursue her graduate degree, get married, and start a family. The familiar question hovered in her mind, *But how?*

The Lord brought clarity to Christine and others for the next steps of Freedom 4/24. Some new yeses presented themselves. By 2010, Christine felt a heightened need to step down as president. She believed someone else with different strengths could take the organization further. As Christine listened to God, she stepped down as president. Her decision to leave the president's position created space for someone else to say yes to God. The board named a new president, Christine would say yes to the invitation to be a board member, and eventually she would even step off the board and simply be known as the founder and advocate. Christine also said yes to being a wife and mom, graduating with her master's degree, and supporting other local ministries. Freedom 4/24 continues to grow, and today more people are experiencing the joy of leadership in that kingdom work.

When we are open to yes and take that first small step, we should be prepared for the wild adventure that God will take us on. There will be questions. We may not know where it will take us. And when it doesn't feel safe, the Holy Spirit will be our safety belt, keeping us close to Jesus as we go on the ride. The Spirit will shape us, bring us what we need, and take all that we give him to create something beautiful for his kingdom . . . and inside of us too.

SMALL STEPS WITH STRENGTHS

King David started small, quite literally. Compared to his older and stronger brothers, he was the smallest in stature. And although he may have been the youngest, God gave him some tremendous talent. As is often the case, this talent wasn't fully realized right away, and neither was the purpose for it. David said yes to use his God-given strengths one step at a time.

The story begins in 1 Samuel 16 with a man named Saul who was king of Israel. He made one mistake after another and continued to dishonor God. The Lord told the prophet Samuel that there would be a new king for Israel, and it would be Samuel's assignment to anoint the next ruler. The Lord revealed little detail on who or when, only that this new king would come from Jesse's clan. Jesse was a farmer and sheep breeder in Bethlehem. Samuel listened to the Lord and trekked to Bethlehem to anoint this unknown future king.

Samuel approached Jesse, the father of eight sons, to choose the next king of Israel. Samuel, and everyone else, assumed that God would choose one of the big and strong sons who had some life experience. When Jesse presented Samuel with seven of his sons who fit this description, the Lord told Samuel that none of these men fit the bill. Samuel asked if other sons remained. Jesse replied, "There is still the youngest, . . . but he's out in the fields watching the sheep and goats" (1 Samuel 16:11). Surely the little shepherd boy wasn't the next king of Israel.

His father had assigned him the challenging and unglamorous work of tending sheep. A good shepherd would go after the one lost sheep and bring it back, due to the sheep's vulnerability. Many predators waited to kill the sheep. The shepherd protected the flock from these enemies, fending the hunters off in whatever manner he could. God saw David's faithfulness in tending his father's sheep. The Lord had entrusted David with the task of caring for these helpless animals and leading them to good pasture. David invested in the flock God had given him as a young boy, even though it came with little fanfare.

David likely didn't know that the humility, faithfulness, and bravery he'd developed with his flocks in the field would be the same strengths with which he would one day shepherd the people of Israel.

Samuel anointed David as king in a private ceremony with his family. It would not be public until much later (2 Samuel 2:4, 5:3), as Saul was still on the throne and would not take kindly to this succession plan.

In Samuel 16:14-23, we learn that King Saul continued to have troubles. An unrelenting spirit tormented him, and Saul heard that a young shepherd boy named David played the harp. The harp was well-known for its soothing music. Word began to travel that David possessed good judgment, brave character, and that the Lord was with him. Perhaps this shepherd boy could help drive these spirits away. Saul invited David to help him, and the shepherd boy accepted the challenge. The combination of David's music and the presence of God helped drive the tormenting spirits away whenever they plagued Saul. David quickly gained favor with the king, and it was known all the more that David was close to God.

Again, David said yes to use his strengths in small ways, which later led to greater influence. Little did David know that God would continue to grow his creative gifts and love for the Lord. This would result in David writing over seventy Psalms, which are documented in the Bible and have led people into worship and intimacy with God for centuries.

Then in Samuel 17, we discover the Philistine army in battle with the Israelites. In particular, a bully named Goliath belonged to the Philistine army. He enjoyed tormenting the Israelite troops.

Did I mention he was nine feet tall?

For forty days Goliath taunted and threatened the Israelites. King Saul and his army shook with fear as they faced this giant every day. Surely if they ventured over the battle line, they would be killed instantly.

Enter the young shepherd boy, David. His father wanted him to go check in on his brothers in the army. Before David left, he made sure someone else would take care of his sheep, and then, bearing gifts of food for the troops, David appeared before King Saul and the army. When David witnessed Goliath's threats, anger boiled inside his soul, "Who is this pagan Philistine anyway, that he is allowed to defy the armies of the living God?" (1 Samuel 17:26).

I can only imagine what the rest of the army felt as they saw this young boy waltz in with such arrogance. As if he would understand how to get rid of this beast of a solider. His brothers voiced this irritation, telling him to go back to tending sheep.

Perhaps this wasn't arrogance on David's part. Maybe the Lord incited righteous anger in David—anger that the Lord's people were being humiliated, and their fear became larger than their faith in God.

David took the opportunity to put his faith into action—as well as his practiced skills to protect and fight for his flock. He asked Saul for permission to battle Goliath. Miraculously, using the tools he felt comfortable with—his shepherd's staff, sling, and five smooth stones—David took down the bully. The Philistine soldiers turned and ran for their lives.

The fight with Goliath embodied more than a showdown with a tyrant. This grew David's confidence in the Lord's power and his heart for the Israelites. As king, David would need faith that God's presence would go with him and his people, even in seemingly impossible circumstances.

In David's journey with God, he discovered the talents the Lord gave him that proved to be very helpful to people and his future kingdom. God used those early yeses to stretch the legs of David's leadership, influence, and faith.

You may not be asked to be the next king of Israel, but it's likely that God has plans for you that are much bigger than you realize in your current moment. Choosing to say yes and develop your talents in smaller ways now may lead to a bigger yes in the future. Discovering the gifts God gave you is one thing, but believing you possess them is quite another.

What strength do you notice God using in your life repeatedly? How might this be preparing you for a greater yes?

EVERYONE HAS SOMETHING

I believe everyone has at least one—and likely many more—talent. This isn't just a belief but a promise from God. It is written in Ephesians 2:10, "We are God's master-piece. He has created us anew in Christ Jesus, so we can do the good things he planned for us long ago."

All of us are God's masterpieces. *Imago Dei*, made in the image of God, is unique to humans as written in the creation account of Genesis 1 and 2. God made both women and men in his image, and all ethnicities bear his image as well. As image bearers of God, we reflect his love and are deeply loved by the Lord, our Creator. When he made humans, God deemed us all "very good."

Alas, no one is perfect, and we live in an imperfect world. We have all fallen short of the glory of God (Romans 3:23). We need forgiveness and healing through the only one who can give it, Jesus Christ. When we surrender our lives to him, transformation occurs. We are made new. We gain superpowers in the form of spiritual gifts. Our rough edges become smoother with the redemptive power of Jesus. We gain fulfillment in Christ rather than in other people or external rewards. We begin living and thinking differently. This transformation overflows from our lives and into the world . . . a world that desperately needs hope and restoration.

In God's design, he has given all of us "good things" to do which he "planned for us long ago." When he created you, he not only made a masterpiece but also planned for you to do something— something good. This something will help bring healing to the world and bring God's kingdom that much closer to earth. It will bring tremendous joy to your spirit as you partner with God and live into your purpose because it's what you were made for.

These good things to do are different for everyone. They are unique to you and your life. It is pointless to compare because God operates on a completely different scale. He has the power to multiply the smallest "good thing" in his kingdom. What seems small to us, is often very big to God.

SMALL GIFT, BIG INFLUENCE

In the mid-1970s, Mary was a sixty-nine-year-old widow in Cleveland, Ohio. Through a church missionary, she learned about a young Rwandan named Célestin, who converted to Christianity and had leadership potential. He attended a Baptist secondary school in Cyimbili, Rwanda, studied Christian education, and received mentoring in evangelism and discipleship. While Célestin enjoyed his studies and growing in Christ, his decision to follow the supreme living God rather than the gods of his ancestors came at a price. His family and village disowned him, which gave him little to no resources to put himself through school. On many occasions Célestin begged for food, ate from the garbage, and slept under bridges.

Mary desired to support this young man and his growing vision to bring the good news of Christ to more people in Rwanda. There was a slight problem in that Mary lacked finances too. How could this poor widow in Cleveland, Ohio, help this Rwandan student with promise and vision?

Mary took a small step and became resourceful. She had the ability and time to collect recyclable trash along the side of the road and turn it in for cash. The amount totaled between six and seven dollars per month. In faith, she regularly sent this money to Célestin through the missionary who had led him to Christ. Mary's gifts supplied Célestin's living expenses, fees, and school uniform, without which he would not have been allowed in school.

In 1979, as Célestin finished secondary school, he felt the call to be a Christian minister and go back to his home village, which had rejected him and God. This would be a difficult mission, but his church agreed and sent him to Rwanguba Bible Institute in Congo (former Zaire), where he spent four years in theological training. Mary's donations of six or seven dollars per month continued to support Célestin through Bible school.

Célestin did move back to his village to begin his pastoral ministry. Within three years he witnessed his whole family coming to know Christ, along with many in his village! Célestin then became involved with community development and leadership training through his denomination, which led to several moves, including one to Kenya, where he studied theology and prepared to train national leaders.

In 1994, the Rwandan genocide broke out. In the space of one hundred days, between five hundred thousand and one million Rwandans were killed at the hands of the militias—70 percent of Rwandan pastors were killed or forced into exile in the genocide. Many of these pastors had hidden endangered people in homes and church sanctuaries. It was an unthinkable tragedy in Célestin's home country, and he felt called to be part of the efforts to heal the devastation. He knew that there was much work to do in discovering how something like this could happen in the first place, and then rebuilding a theological foundation, which would prevent this from happening again. Rwanda had experienced a decrease in strong biblical teaching, and instead of people giving their loyalty to Jesus Christ, they identified with tribes and political figures who were calling them to kill one another. Célestin founded ALARM, African Leadership and Reconciliation Ministries, which develops servant leaders who reconcile and transform lives affected by conflict and injustice, all in the name of Christ. Today, ALARM has touched the lives of thousands across East Africa, and Rwandans continue to rebuild on the cornerstone of Jesus.

There is much more to say about Célestin and ALARM, and you can find more information on their website www.alarm-inc .org, but let's circle back to Mary's "something." The small good thing that God had planned for her to do in that season of life was to collect just enough money to contribute toward Célestin's living expenses, school fees, and uniform. Célestin could not have made it through secondary school without the supplemental income Mary had provided. And while Célestin never met Mary, she became a mother to him in many ways. It may be no coincidence that Mary died several days after Célestin graduated.

Mary could not have known that her small step would enable this future dynamic leader to earn his degree in theology and then use that degree to teach thousands what it means to live, lead, and love like Jesus. Mary didn't know she would be part of changing the culture not only in Rwanda but in eight other East African countries as well. I wish I could ask Mary how her giving of these gifts changed her and what she learned about God in the process. We often grow in big ways through our small steps.

What could be a small yes for you to help heal a place of injustice in the world?

SPIRITUAL EXPERIMENT

Take a spiritual gifts assessment to discover more of the unique strengths God has given you. Discuss your top five strengths with your small group or other trusted friends. Reflect on how God may be growing these strengths in a yes he may have for you.

Chapter Five

· ·

GROWING THROUGH YOUR YES

Teddi and her family piled into their SUV, left the suburbs, and ventured forty-five minutes toward the city's downtown district. They'd planned a family fun night, which included a picnic while cheering on the local baseball team. It was one of those beautiful, idyllic spring evenings. The scents of spring flowers hung in the air, the grass began to burst with green again, and the sun thawed the last bit of frost from the ground. Teddi's family arrived downtown and snagged a parking spot in a nearby gravel lot. The evening held promise for good family bonding.

As they hustled from the parking lot to the baseball game, they passed several homeless people holding signs. One sign captured Teddi's eye. It read, "Do you have a sandwich?" She had never seen a sign with such a specific request. Teddi entered the baseball park and saw a crowd full of families like hers, rolling coolers filled with snacks, beverages, and sandwiches.

While baseballs were pitched and the crowd cheered, Teddi continued thinking about this sign. *All he wants is someone's extra peanut butter and jelly sandwich. We can do that. That seems easy.*

*Once the kids are out of school for the summer, we could pack sack
lunches of peanut butter and jelly sandwiches and bring them to people
who are hungry.*

Teddi attempted to be present with her family that evening,
but her thoughts kept moving toward this mission, which I will
refer to as "Operation PB&J." She could sense her excitement
building. This could actually happen. She needed to tell her
husband and get him on board.

After the outing, Teddi discussed her PB&J idea with her
husband. He expressed a lot of concerns. He thought it was too
dangerous for his wife and three children to go downtown and interact with this population. Who knows what they would encounter?

"Yep, you're right. It's a dumb idea. What was I thinking?"
Teddi agreed and decided not to pursue it. Instead she resumed
her summer plans of vacation Bible school, kids' sports teams, and
days at the pool.

Months later, Teddi read *Just Courage* by Gary Haugen, president of International Justice Mission. The book encouraged her
to embody courage instead of fear when pursuing God and opportunities he may provide. This, combined with a sermon series
at her church entitled Brave Not Safe made Teddi's soul restless.
The memory of the sandwich sign flooded her heart again. She
prayed for God to help her pitch this idea to her husband one
more time.

God had been leading Teddi's husband on his own journey
during this time, including a mission trip to Honduras. God
softened his heart toward the world around him. When Teddi
approached him with the idea a second time, he was ready. Before
long, the family had packed dozens of sack lunches.

As Teddi prayed and listened to God, she sensed a clear vision
from him to go to a downtown park across from the central library.

Teddi loaded up her SUV with kids and sandwiches. As they neared the park, her nervousness increased.

Teddi said, "I never had such butterflies as the first day we did this. I thought, *What am I doing?!* I had never done anything like this before. I didn't feel unsafe, but I was concerned how the people we served would receive this. What if it didn't mean anything to them?"

On her first couple of trips to the park, the homeless people didn't really care. While they took the sandwiches, there was little communication. *Perhaps the sandwiches are missing the mark? Was this a bad idea?* Teddi thought.

Teddi and her kids showed up every Tuesday morning at 11:30 with sandwiches, week after week, whether it rained, sweltered with heat, or snowed. Trust built between Teddi and the homeless community at the park.

She left judgment at the door as they passed out lunches. They gained empathy as they listened to people and heard their stories. She started to get to know people and to connect with them. She shared this story:

> The sweetest man showed up every week. He was in jail for unspeakable things. I never asked about his past, but I knew he had been in prison for twenty years. He was kind to my children and me. We took his laundry home and washed it. We brought him detergent the next time we saw him so he could do his own laundry too. We built a friendship with him.

Teddi grew tremendously in this yes to God. She grew in her dependence on God to take this risk and step out of her comfort zone. She grew in prayer as she prayed for God to work through her and her kids as they handed out PB&J. Teddi grew in her love for this marginalized, homeless population at the park. She saw God's heart overlap with hers.

"I never knew I could receive so much joy from making and serving sandwiches. I literally felt the breath of God on my neck. That's how close I felt to his Spirit when we were with our friends at the park," Teddi maintained.

Teddi did not expect profound intimacy with Christ to grow in her through this yes. This is what happens, however, when we partner with Jesus. We feel the breath of God on our necks.

When we partner with Jesus, we feel the breath of God on our necks.

Teddi couldn't keep this amazing blessing to herself. She began inviting other moms and their children to join her. More sandwiches were made, and more people experienced blessing in the receiving and the giving. Eventually, her church caught wind of what they were doing and offered to make the sandwiches by enlisting help from even more families. It became a community of yes.

For seven years on every Tuesday at 11:30 a.m., Teddi anchored her yes in Christ, continued to be obedient, and brought others with her on the journey. It wasn't always easy as she encountered other people's mistrust of her motivations and actions. Others told her she only perpetuated the "bad behavior" of this population, and she should leave the park. Teddi reflected, "In the midst of my anger, I remembered truth from Scripture. God calls us to be different. When we are different, we are countercultural, and it is not always well received," Teddi said.

Eventually, the time did come when Teddi felt God's invitation to say no to this particular ministry, at least for a season. She needed to trust that God would continue to minister to her friends in the park.

As Teddi wrestled with letting go, she began to understand why God had drawn her to the park in the first place. It wasn't the desire to feed the homeless, although that was a blessing. The real longing inside of Teddi was to extend love and dignity to people in the margins because she knew firsthand what it was like to be there. At eighteen years old she'd found herself unexpectedly pregnant, unmarried, and receiving loads of judgment from others. At eighteen, it would have been nice to have more people extend kindness and grace.

As Teddi reflected on her time at the park, she realized the significance of her life story and the importance of this yes God had uniquely given her. Perhaps healing and redemption can take place through something as simple as a peanut butter and jelly sandwich.

PARTNERSHIP IN YES

God gave Deborah opportunity to say yes in unprecedented ways. The fourth chapter in the book of Judges states that she was a prophetess and judge in a season before there were kings in Israel. While there had been notable women earlier in the Old Testament, Deborah was the first woman to hold this kind of positional and influential leadership.

From what Judges 4:5 describes, the Lord gave Deborah much favor and wisdom as she led Israel. The people freely went to her for advice as she sat under a designated palm tree known as the Palm of Deborah. They knew she heard from the Lord, and they trusted her guidance.

As we enter the story, we read that Israel had rebelled against God yet again, and as a consequence the Lord gave them over to an oppressive Canaanite, King Jabin, for twenty years. Life under King Jabin's rule continued to be unbearable, and the Israelites cried out to God for help.

The Lord revealed to Deborah that he would make a way for Israel to become free. God told Deborah to prepare one of their soldiers, Barak, for the task. Deborah obeyed and told Barak that the Lord commanded him to take ten thousand men to fight the army of Jabin, led by the commander, Sisera. Deborah assured Barak that God would give him victory, and all of Israel would finally be free.

This makes good sense. Deborah used her gifts of discernment and leadership to share God's vision with a capable soldier, who could then recruit an army for battle. She handed the task to Barak, and she could return to the palm tree.

But Barak would not go without Deborah.

The people greatly respected her for her intimacy with God and the wisdom that flowed from her. Barak may have had the physical stature to lead ten thousand men into battle, but he wanted Deborah's godly insight and leadership to guide these men.

Unconventional doesn't begin to describe this situation. Women were not asked to help in military matters. Then again, there weren't any other women judges ruling the Middle East, either.

It takes courage and confidence in God to be open to yes when the invitation goes against cultural norms. Deborah was anchored in her faith and likely passionate about seeing her people set free. I'm certain she longed for the Israelites to repent of their rebellion and desired the freedom that would follow. If she could play a part in leading her people out of this oppression, she would say yes, even if this partnership with Barak seemed crazy.

Have you ever said yes to something that seemed odd to others?

Deborah readily agreed to go with Barak. She said, "Very well, I will go with you. But you will receive no honor in this venture, for the LORD's victory over Sisera will be at the hands of a woman" (Judges 4:9).

On first read we may think Deborah was shaming Barak for his insecurity and lack of faith. We could assume his cowardice led him to request the help of Deborah to lead his army. As a result of his disobedience, a woman would get the honor of this victory and not him. We could easily infer that this woman is Deborah, given her role and authority in this scene. Perhaps our own unconscious gender role biases might play a part in this interpretation as well.

Another interpretation to consider is that Barak was not being disobedient but was instead embodying humility and great faith. He knew he had talent in leading an army, but he did not want to take on the monumental battle without the wisdom and discernment of God. After all, Israel's freedom was at stake, and it had already been a long twenty years. He knew Deborah's strengths and that his army would need her help.

It's similar to Moses telling God in Exodus 33 that his presence was needed to get to the Promised Land. Moses said, "If you don't personally go with us, don't make us leave this place. How will anyone know that you look favorably on me—on me and on your people—if you don't go with us? For your presence among us sets your people and me apart from all other people on the earth" (Exodus 33: 15-16).

Barak's ego didn't need recognition for Israel's upcoming victory. He desired God's power and presence to go with them, and he wanted Israel free. God's glory mattered more than his reputation. In fact, Barak is named in Hebrews 11 with other great examples of faith. Perhaps Deborah was not shaming but more encouraging his act of humility and naming the trust in God it took for him to invite Deborah into this yes with him.

Deborah and Barak teach us important lessons as we partner with each other in a yes. They named the talent the other possessed.

They were not threatened or envious of each other's skills. Deborah and Barak empowered one another to use these strengths to accomplish the goal set before them. And if they had any unconscious biases, they seemed uncovered—for themselves and one another. They needed each other to grow this yes toward Israel's victory and freedom, and they honored one another in the process.

As my pastor says, "A community of yes is a powerful force." Not only can we have more impact with a variety of resources being used, but if we humble ourselves, we learn from one another too. A powerful testimony may result if God's people embolden one another instead of compete, and uplift each other instead of undercut.

May we take courage for ourselves and make room for each other as we find and grow our yeses together.

GROWTH THROUGH INVITING OTHERS

"I'm so excited to lead a Bible study in my fraternity! Mark is going to teach me how to get it started and let me know when I'm ready to go for it!"

These are not words I hear every day. In fact, I never hear these words.

When Rick, a nineteen-year-old college sophomore, introduced himself to me, I wondered where he came from. I led campus ministry at the university Rick attended, and he recently had discovered our group. Rick oozed energy and his face beamed with joy. He could hardly contain his enthusiasm as he sat across from me in the student union.

Curiosity got the best of me, and I asked to hear more of his story.

Rick proceeded to tell me what his life had been like growing up. He shared about the bad decisions he'd made in recent years: the drugs and alcohol he chose to numb the pain, which became addictions as he ran with the wild crowd. He joined the army and continued his lifestyle. He wanted nothing to do with Jesus. But when he hit rock bottom, the army chaplain took him under his wing. Tired of running from past hurts, Rick knew there had to be more to life. As he understood more about Jesus and his lavish grace to extend forgiveness and love, Rick was hooked. He began running after Jesus, consuming Scripture, and making choices that honored God. His life radically changed as he said yes to Jesus.

"When I left the army and enrolled at Purdue, I wanted to not only go to classes, I also wanted others to know about Jesus."

Rick joined a fraternity on campus, and he desired to spread this great news of Christ to his new brothers. Did I mention that Rick's fraternity had not seen the likes of a Bible study before? This yes would require a lot of prayer.

And pray we did. The first year Rick led the study, very few people attended. He would post signs in the house, and they would get ripped apart. Many of his brothers ridiculed him. Rick continued to say yes, even though the results weren't what he'd hoped. He faithfully met with my colleague and me for mentoring and training. He persevered in praying for and loving his fraternity brothers.

The second year, Tom joined Rick's fraternity. Rick intentionally recruited Tom to his fraternity because he'd heard of Tom's faithfulness to Christ. Rick cast his vision for sharing Jesus with his brothers and seeing a more positive culture grow in the house as a result. What if God could renew this fraternity?

Who could you invite to partner with you in a yes?

Tom decided to join Rick in this audacious yes. The two of them met with me for mentoring that year. During one of our appointments, Tom and Rick expressed in frustration how hard it was to keep being faithful to Jesus with so much opposition from their brothers. We studied the book of Acts that semester, and we happened to be in Acts 5 that day. As we read about Peter and John leading the early church while the religious authorities opposed them, Tom and Rick perked up. Their vision expanded as they read about thousands of people deciding to follow Christ, even in the midst of Peter and John being flogged for their leadership. Peter and John's yes inspired Tom and Rick's yes.

Through tears, I said, "Guys, what you've decided to do is harder than we thought. Sometimes I wonder what we're asking eighteen- to twenty-two-year-olds to do. Is it too much?"

Though they appreciated my empathic heart, I learned a lot from Tom and Rick that day. They answered back, "We are doing what God has called us to do! We're just like Peter and John! We're going to rejoice that God has counted us worthy to suffer disgrace for the name of Jesus!" (see Acts 5:41). And with that they gave each other high fives, filled with a renewed hope. God knew what he was doing as Tom and Rick encouraged each other in their yes that semester.

And their ministry grew little by little. A few people would attend their Bible study, which was now termed a GIG (Group Investigating God). People felt free to come as they were . . . skeptics, questions, and doubts were all welcome. God began to break through the tough exterior of some brothers, and there seemed to be some openness among people.

Then Rick and Tom decided to invite brothers to a conference that our ministry hosts, one specifically geared for fraternity and sorority students. This conference helps students take the next step in their relationship with Christ, no matter where they are in their faith journey. Rick and Tom brought over twenty brothers to this conference. Many decided to follow Christ in new and fresh ways!

We were all floored to say the least. God simply showed off at this point! This spiritual momentum carried through for several years as the GIG had so many people attend that they had to sit in the stairway to listen in.

Tom invited one of the brothers, Chris, to the discussion group. He knew Chris had questions about God and needed a safe place to wrestle with them. After attending the group for several months, Chris's life transformed as he said yes to Jesus. God's love changed him so much, he eventually joined Rick and Tom in their yes to lead ministry in the fraternity.

How could you help someone find their first yes to Jesus?

Years later, as I attended the weddings of these men, my heart soared with delight. They had chosen each other to stand as witnesses in these sacred life moments, just as they stood with one another in their fraternity. At each wedding we reminisced about God's glory working through them and recounted gratitude for one another.

Today, each man continues to build on his yes from college. Rick leads an urban ministry for disenfranchised teenagers. Tom is an engineer who seeks to honor Christ in the marketplace and in a local urban church ministry. Chris has a career in finance and enjoys helping others multiply and steward their resources in generous ways. Each of these men said yes, along with their wives, to raising their children in the ways of Christ. They hope to see a new generation of kingdom leaders grow up and say yes to hard and good things. Who would have thought Rick's one, unlikely yes inside of the fraternity would spread this far and wide? Only God could know.

DEBRIEF AND INTERPRET

As we find a yes, God grows our character and the invitation to expand beyond our own selves. He allows others the opportunity to get in on the joy of this journey too. What I have discovered is that it's easy to miss these rich growth opportunities if I'm not intentional to slow down and pay attention to what the Spirit is doing . . . and saying . . . in the midst of the activity.

The practice of debriefing can go a long way in helping us to press pause and mine for the gems in this midst of our doing. InterVarsity Christian Fellowship has developed a model I find helpful called the Discipleship Cycle. The cycle has three parts: hear the word, respond actively, and debrief and interpret.

Our yes is inspired by and centered in God's truth from Scripture. Next, we respond to his invitations and do the work. Lastly, and perhaps most importantly, we debrief. Debriefing helps us reflect on what it is that God is doing in us and in others as we engage with him in the work he has given us. It's not always obvious to see, as the evidence for growth may lie beneath the surface of our activity.

I have a few go-to questions that help me open up to the learning God has for me and the transformation he may want to do in me:

- What am I noticing about myself?
- What am I noticing in others?
- What am I learning about God?
- What might God be saying to me as a result?

Pretty simple. It's startling to me how a few words can provoke deep thoughts if I give it some time.

These questions help me reflect individually and also cultivate good conversation with people who are on a particular yes journey with me. As I seek to interpret what these answers mean, the questions change to prayer prompts. If I can still my body and quiet my mind for a few minutes, the Holy Spirit will reveal to me more than just my initial answers. He often will enlighten my heart to why something has stood out to me, and perhaps why I need to learn more about him in this area of my life. In those quiet moments of an intentional pause, he often speaks if I'm willing to listen. These are the gems of the debrief and the jewels of our yes.

It is here in the debrief that I frequently think of who else I could bring with me as I do this activity again. Who would be blessed to receive some of these rich treasures? By inviting someone to join me, I am not implying that I am an expert on this path. I am simply asking someone to join me as I join Jesus. Perhaps my invitation is the encouragement someone needs to take their own step of faith. Just as I had obstacles to this yes, others will have obstacles too. It's easier to clear the hurdles when we have people cheering us on.

God wired us to have meaningful connection with him and with others. Our yes may very well be a conduit to these connections. So, in the words of the modern-day poet Ferris Bueller, "Life moves pretty fast. If you don't stop and look around once in a while, you could miss it."

Let's not miss the abundance God has for us on the adventure—and for those we journey alongside.

SPIRITUAL EXPERIMENT

Practice inviting someone to join you in your yes. Consider role-playing the invite with a friend. Think through possible obstacles someone might have. How could you encourage their openness to yes?

....

Part Two

STAYING
WITH YOUR
YES

Chapter Six

YES ... BUT

Your son has autism."

With this one sentence, Mike and Jennifer Wiese's world jolted off its axis. Their oldest son was diagnosed at age seven with this complicated condition, and they needed help. It was 2002, and Mike and Jennifer strapped on their learning hats, scouring the country for the best resources to navigate this new path. They longed for their son to have the opportunity to live to his fullest potential.

They landed in Vancouver at an autism conference. There they attended presentations on methods to assist those with the condition, many of which were expensive—and experimental. However, one possibility piqued Mike and Jennifer's curiosity. Research revealed a correlation between gluten-free foods and improving autism symptoms. Although they knew nothing about gluten-free foods, Jennifer enjoyed cooking, and this seemed to be a doable option for their family of six.

Armed with hope and gluten-free recipes, Jennifer and Mike left Vancouver and marched into their local grocery store to collect the necessary ingredients. Discouragement quickly descended as they scanned the scanty supply. Even so, they gathered what they could and whipped up a few of the recipes, only to discover they all tasted terrible. It seemed highly unlikely that four boys under the age of seven would rally around this new diet. They had to find something more palatable.

So Jennifer put her joy of cooking to work and transformed her kitchen into a laboratory. She experimented in hopes of inventing a gluten-free flour mix. Such a mix would allow her to concoct all sorts of baked goods. Wouldn't it be great for her son to go to his next birthday party with a treat he could eat? Furthermore, wouldn't it be wonderful if everyone else enjoyed it too?

Time was limited in their household. The family's car dealership required much of Mike's time, and Jennifer had her hands full managing their young and vibrant boys. But Jennifer started small and enjoyed using her gluten-free flour to treat her family. They loved it. So did their friends. As Jennifer's son continued to bring gluten-free cupcakes to birthday parties, the parents began requesting more and more of her treats.

YES, BUT IT'S SLOW

By 2008, Jennifer had created pizza dough, cupcakes, cookies, and breads. With the encouragement of her family and friends, Jennifer decided to bake for resale, not just her family. She then looked for a commercial kitchen to rent. A local restaurant owner heard of Jennifer's vision, and she offered her kitchen to Jennifer. The restaurant owner told Jennifer, "Someone took a chance on me when I started this business. I want to pay it forward and invest in you."

Fueled by all this support, Jennifer took a leap of faith and landed a spot in the local farmers' market. While Jennifer's soul filled with excitement, she still battled her own obstacles to yes. *I'm a stay-at-home mom, not a businesswoman. I don't know enough about this industry. What am I doing?*

Despite her doubts about herself, she realized God was slowly opening doors for her. She needed to be patient and trust his timing. This would be a slow journey. Jennifer had a house full of boys to raise and limited time. Her husband was more than busy with his career in the family business. This yes had already been six years in the making. She needed to take one step at time and see what God would do.

What invitations from God do you need to trust his timing for?

Jennifer reflected, "I owed it to myself and my children to take a chance and try. I wanted to model this for my kids. We keep telling them to take risks and pursue their dreams. I thought, if I don't do this, what does that communicate?"

Jennifer thoroughly enjoyed the farmers' market, and the consumers reciprocated that joy. Her gluten-free treats proved to be popular. She began to find more time to invest in this hobby, and it seemed to bless others. God continued to give Jennifer confidence as he reminded her of her story. She did have a business degree. She even had a sales job right out of college. A strong work ethic combined with entrepreneurship ran through her family tree as well. Jennifer realized she did possess the skills needed for this adventure.

By 2012, Mike and Jennifer's life was full of teenage boys and stress. Mike's business had taken several downturns due to a change in partnerships and the 2008 economic crash. He began to wonder whether this was where God wanted him to be. It was a frightening thought at the age of fifty-two. Jennifer's budding food hobby served as a nice distraction from his stress. He enjoyed helping her create marketing strategies and suggesting next steps she could take in her business venture. Jennifer now sold to several local vendors, and their CrossFit group asked them to come up with a paleo-friendly snack beyond beef jerky or almonds. Warrior Mix evolved from their kitchen and found a happy home with not only their CrossFit friends but with other CrossFit gyms across the city.

By 2013, Mike faced a painful intersection in life. The only job he had ever known caused incredible stress. His family and his health were being impacted. He and Jennifer prayed, discussed, and prayed some more. They finally decided to take another leap of faith, and Mike left his career with the auto dealership. While relief flooded his soul, so did grief and anxiety. What on earth would he do now in this stage of life? What did he really want to do? That was an intriguing and new question for Mike to entertain.

As Mike pondered the question of what he wanted in life, a few values came to the surface. He and Jennifer enjoyed working together when they could. Their family needed to be a priority no matter which path he chose. He wanted to utilize his decades of business acumen. As things settled for Mike, he and Jennifer both became excited about working together to build Warrior Mix and the other baked goods. They held a vision to help people be healthy in order to live their best life . . . the life God has for them. This was the same vision they'd had for their oldest son all those years ago in Vancouver. Now it would be a vision for people across the country.

Mike's visionary and marketing skills, combined with Jennifer's creativity and networking talent, produced BeeFree Gluten-Free Bakery. This would be their yes, and they committed to be all in with one another and this invitation from God.

Surely this process would move fast, now that they had all this time to devote to their yes. They needed it to move fast. Their oldest son's college education loomed around the corner, with the other three following close behind. And there was no paycheck to be found in these early days of yes.

Mike and Jennifer hustled. It was exciting and invigorating to see interest from buyers and local grocery chains.

Then the bottom fell out. Within six months, Jennifer's dad was diagnosed with terminal cancer and her mom was diagnosed with stage 4 cancer. The grief was overwhelming, and priorities shifted in a heartbeat. Their yes would have to slow down, yet again.

What are we doing? Have we completely lost our minds? How will we make our car payment this month? Did we hear from God correctly? These were the thoughts that came to Jennifer's mind.

It was in some of these distressed moments God would provide a grocery store chain to put their baked goods on their shelves. Then another order would trickle in to cover that month's cost. Though they had fears and unexpected bumps in the road, God provided for them.

Jennifer's dad eventually passed away, but her mother survived. Mike and Jennifer's faith continued to grow as they learned to trust God in the midst of the waiting. Waiting for healing and waiting for death. Waiting for paychecks and waiting on grocery stores. Waiting for God to reveal more of this yes and waiting for his hope.

Jennifer reflected on the development of her trust in God during this waiting. "I can't imagine God would bring us this far to fail. And if it does crumble, then it's because God has something better. I have to believe that, because if I don't believe in that, I don't believe in anything."

With open hands and pressing on toward yes, Mike and Jennifer received a great gift. After eighteen months of pursuing buyers at Kroger grocery stores, Warrior Mix hit the shelves! After two years of perseverance, Warrior Mix found a home at Meijer. A nine-month wait resulted in Target stocking Warrior Mix too.

Now Warrior Mix is at most leading grocery chains across the country, along with the convenient amazon.com. Mike and Jennifer's yes took seventeen years to come into full vision. That vision continues to grow and expand for BeeFree's Warrior Mix and the Wiese family.

The invitation God gives us often grows alongside our own journey with Jesus. May we be patient with the journey and ourselves as we wait on God's timing and lean into all that he has for us along the way.

YES, BUT NOT YET

It's not easy to wait on God. In fact, it can be downright painful and confusing. The Lord must have known how difficult this would be for us because the Bible contains many stories of people who had to wait on a yes from God. It's a difficult journey, and it's not always done perfectly. Okay . . . it's not ever done perfectly.

The story of God's promise to Abram and Sarai (later known as Abraham and Sarah) is one example we have in Scripture of finding such a yes. God asked Abram and Sarai to be major players in God's kingdom story. In their yes, God invited Abram and Sarai into relationship with him. They learned how to trust him in the midst of the obstacles to yes.

Invitation to trust. It begins in Genesis 12:1-4 when the Lord calls out to Abram:

> "Leave your native country, your relatives, and your father's family, and go to the land that I will show you. I will make you into a great nation. I will bless you and make you famous, and you will be a blessing to others. I will bless those who bless you and curse those who treat you with contempt. All the families on earth will be blessed through you."

So Abram departed as the LORD had instructed.

We can read this and think it all sounds so easy. God spoke to Abram. God gave him a promise. God instructed him to move. Abram was obedient. Done and done.

This text gives little detail of what is happening in the background and how people are feeling. If we put ourselves in the middle of the story with the characters, curiosity can begin to bubble within us, which can lead to good questions and deeper meaning.

Here are some facts to frame this story:

- Abram was seventy-five years old (Gen. 12:4).

- His wife, Sarai, was not able to have children (Gen. 11:30), and she was sixty-five years old.

- The couple settled in the town of Haran in ancient Mesopotamia. They had previously traveled six hundred miles from the city of Ur, also in Mesopotamia (Gen. 11:31), with Abram's father and nephew. Abram's dad died.

- God spoke to Abram. God had not interacted with humans for nine generations, since the Tower of Babel incident (Genesis 11).

As I put myself in Abram and Sarai's shoes, I begin to wonder what the conversation between the two of them was that evening:

SARAI. Let me get this straight. You heard from God, personally?

ABRAM. Yes, dear. I've told you this a hundred times. God spoke to me.

SARAI. Just to clarify, God not only spoke to you, but he told you that we have to leave everything we know? Just walk away?

ABRAM. That's correct.

SARAI. And God said he would make you into a great nation that blesses you and others, all families on earth will be blessed through you? How might a nation come from you when your wife is infertile and we are older than dirt? And how do we know this is really God you are hearing from?

ABRAM. I have no idea. I'm just as confused as you are!

SARAI. I guess we won't be retiring anytime soon.

Certainly, there is no proof that this conversation existed. I doubt there was such a term as retirement, either. Becoming curious about how they may have felt helps me relate to Abram and Sarai as they face this invitation from God. It's not an easy invite. In fact, it's downright hard. Abram and Sarai didn't have a track record with God at this point. I can't imagine the faith and courage it took to say yes to this impossible but incredibly compelling vision.

Abram and Sarai packed up and traveled another five hundred miles through the desert. They finally reached the land of Canaan. The area was inhabited by Canaanites, but God promised Abram that this land would be given to him and his descendants. Abram takes him at his word, built an altar to worship God, and commemorated this promise.

After a long journey, I'm sure Abram and Sarai were relieved to find the land they were looking for.

Until the famine hit Canaan.

Once again, Abram and Sarai pack up and move out, this time to Egypt to find food and livelihood. Again, putting myself in the shoes of Abram and Sarai, I wonder what this would have been like:

ABRAM: Are you kidding me? I'm exhausted. This is the land. God told me! Why is there a famine happening?

Sarai: What was the time frame on this promise? When are we meant to have all the land and all the children? This is going to set it back a few years. Does God know how old we are?

Abram and Sarai are learning to trust God in this journey. Waiting will do that. This trust they are developing with the Lord will be the foundation needed for future generations of faithfulness. However, sometimes in the waiting we grow impatient and our faith is challenged.

Obstacle to trust. Abram experienced an obstacle to trust as they entered Egypt. He began to panic about a possible situation. He said to Sarai, "Look, you are a very beautiful woman. When the Egyptians see you, they will say, 'This is his wife. Let's kill him; then we can have her!' So please tell them you are my sister. Then they will spare my life and treat me well because of their interest in you" (Genesis 12:11-13).

I really can't imagine what it must have been like to live in this culture. Back then, women didn't have rights and were treated as property. It was acceptable for men to have multiple wives. But I still really wonder what was going through Sarai's mind as Abram laid out this strategy of deception.

As predicted, the Egyptians thought Sarai was gorgeous. Abram claimed her as a sister and received many gifts in return for allowing Sarai to marry Pharaoh.

I'm certain both Abram and Sarai were scared. They were vulnerable in a foreign land, unsure of how they would be treated, or even whether they would live through this scenario. I honestly can't envision how terrified Sarai was as she waved goodbye to her husband, Abram, and was ushered into the king's palace to engage in marital relations with this stranger.

This wasn't what they thought God had invited them into. In fact, this detour to Egypt surely couldn't be in God's plan. Waiting on God to come through and show another way forward may seem pointless, especially when we have reality staring us in the face. In Abram and Sarai's minds, there was no way forward other than to deceive Pharaoh and sacrifice Sarai. But God does impossible things.

What are the obstacles you experience in trusting God with an invitation to yes?

We get impatient in our waiting for God and take matters into our own hands, which doesn't usually end well. Thankfully, God has abundant grace for us. It doesn't mean there aren't consequences for our actions. It does mean that he can redeem anything, and he will continue to give us opportunities to trust him, again and again.

God extended this grace to Abram and Sarai. He sent terrible plagues upon Pharaoh and his household because he'd married Sarai, and she was Abram's wife. Pharaoh figured this out and was irate. He couldn't understand why Abram lied about this and brought mayhem into his land. He demanded they both exit Egypt immediately and even sent some of his men to escort them out.

I find it interesting that Pharaoh acknowledged God's power with the plagues and understood there would be consequences for taking Sarai as his wife. It does make me wonder if Abram had trusted God for the impossible, would Pharaoh have been respectful of Sarai and Abram's marriage? But God was gracious to Abram, even in the midst of his poor decision in Egypt.

Another invitation to trust. The Lord then led the pair back to Canaan, and God said to Abram: "Look as far as you can see in every direction—north and south, east and west. I am giving all this land, as far as you can see, to you and your descendants as a permanent possession. And I will give you so many descendants that, like the dust of the earth, they cannot be counted!" (Genesis 13:14-16).

Abram worshiped God and trusted him for this promise. Again. Even though it looked impossible as there were no children in sight. God did bless them with wealth and land at this point. He had taken care of them in Egypt. Perhaps this promise would still come true.

We read in Genesis 15:1-2, "Some time later, the LORD spoke to Abram in a vision and said to him, 'Do not be afraid, Abram, for I will protect you, and your reward will be great.' But Abram replied, 'O Sovereign LORD, what good are all your blessings when I don't even have a son?'"

Another obstacle to trust. Abram continues to wait on this promise from God that doesn't seem to be happening, and he's getting antsy. He goes on to explain to God that since a son seems to be the missing piece in this promise, one of his servants' children will have to be the heir to his wealth. Abram tells God that's the only outcome possible at this point.

Waiting on God brings out the control freak in the best of us. Abram tries desperately to control the situation by giving God his game plan. I can't count the number of blueprints I've submitted to God—and the number of plans I simply drew up myself and executed on my own. It's easy to forget that God knows: He knows our realities. He knows what we need. He knows how to fulfill this yes he gave you.

God patiently lays out his covenant promise to Abram:

"No, your servant will not be your heir, for you will have a son of your own who will be your heir." Then the LORD took Abram outside and said to him, "Look up into the sky and count the stars if you can. That's how many descendants you will have!"

And Abram believed the LORD, and the LORD counted him as righteous because of his faith. (Genesis 15:4-6)

The Lord proceeded to speak to Abram and reveal more about the promise of the land he was on and that it would be given to him and passed down to all of his descendants. Abram worshiped God and trusted him for this.

Until he got impatient, again. This time Sarai has her moment of angst in the waiting. In Genesis 16, ten years into this journey to yes, Sarai creates a plan to get this promise fulfilled: She wants Abram to marry her Egyptian servant, Hagar. Hagar will then give Abram a son, and the descendants will start to multiply as God said. Abram agrees to this plan, even though God said this wasn't how his promise would be fulfilled. God has grace for Abram and Sarai in their lack of trust, but there are consequences.

The next fifteen years are full of ups and downs for Abram and Sarai. Ishmael is born to Abram and Hagar. Sarai and Hagar have a tumultuous relationship. Abram and Sarai have tension between them. Hagar is exiled and brought back. Abram witnesses injustice and evil in towns around him and learns more about God's judgment, justice, and mercy. There is no denying that in this waiting period, Abram and Sarai understand more of who God is and how to rely on him.

Finally, after twenty-five years of journeying with God in this promise of yes, God gives a son to Abram and Sarai. God changes their names to Abraham (father of many) and Sarah (princess), and their little guy is named Isaac (he laughs). Isaac's name reflects the reaction Sarah had toward being pregnant at ninety years old. She could not believe such a thing. But God made the impossible happen.

The story of Abraham and Sarah is not a straight and clean path to trusting God. And often our yeses to God won't be either. The Lord gave Abraham and Sarah a vision and continued to bring clarity to that vision over the course of twenty-five years.

Even with clarity and a promise from God, the waiting was painful, it stirred doubt, and desperation emerged.

To receive a yes—but not yet—from God, requires loads of grace and grit. In the midst of finding this kind of yes, a deep love and understanding of Christ may be found . . . if we are willing to look for it.

YES, BUT RECALIBRATE

I can't remember a time when I didn't dream about being a mother. As a little girl, I loved my play kitchen in the basement and entertained many imaginative children in my created house. I had baby dolls that simulated human functions, including one memorable doll that seemed to get diaper rash consistently. One would think that would deter me from the world of babies—it did not.

Babysitting, teaching Sunday school, working at a day care . . . these were all ways I continued to invest in my love for children. "You will make a wonderful mother someday" was a familiar phrase I heard. I considered it a great compliment.

My own mother is a beautiful example of motherhood that I hoped to emulate in some small way. She chose to stay at home with my brother and me when we were young, and poured her heart into us. She nurtured, disciplined, and loved us with a generous spirit. She made our home a safe place to return to after the world beat us up a bit. She welcomed our friends and extended hospitality to everyone. Piles of shoes by the front door and a pantry full of our favorite snacks became commonplace in high school.

I couldn't wait to create this kind of home for my own family someday.

As I entered my late twenties, this desire for motherhood continued to develop. Unfortunately, the father of my unborn children had not shown up yet. Anxiety began to swirl around my soul as

I began to feel left behind. Most of my friends were getting married and beginning to think about starting a family. It seemed like being a mom was a good desire. In fact, God encourages people to have children and raise them in his kingdom. I would definitely do that!

But this waiting challenged my patience.

This desire, which I felt God gave me, might have another invitation attached. There may be an invitation to wait on God's timing and release my own. I likely held expectations for time-lines and schedules that needed more of an open hand. Could I say yes to wait and trust God for these children?

I enacted a new plan: I promised to trust God and wait for my chance to be a mom. In the meantime, I would continue to deepen my relationship with him. Surely the more I invested in him, the closer I would get to meeting my future husband and bearing these children I prayed for.

Months turned into years. I entered my thirties and happily hosted countless baby showers. I became a regular at Babies R Us, and Amazon kept asking me if I would be interested in buying similar products to the sippy cups I kept purchasing. I felt conflict in my soul as I celebrated with my friends and considered it a privilege to walk with them in these precious seasons, but I also felt deep despair. It's curious how our souls can house such opposite emotions at once.

I had given my life to Jesus, even working full time as a campus minister. I loved on the college students he gave me. I loved on the friends he surrounded me with. I became an aunt, and my nieces received all of my mama love. My heart felt like it would burst waiting for this yes to become a reality. The love had to go somewhere.

This waiting was getting out of control. It felt like I'd missed the train everyone climbed into ten years ago, and I somehow needed to catch up. Time was of the essence as I reached the age of a high-risk "mature" pregnancy.

To add insult to injury, at age thirty-eight a dating relationship ended, and my body betrayed me. A polyp grew where a baby should have grown, and a handful of tumors kept it company too. I felt miserable, and now I needed surgery, which could affect my ability to have babies. Tears seemed to hover in my throat on any given day.

I ached with longing for this yes to be fulfilled. I didn't sense a no from God, and yet I didn't get an absolute certainty that my desire would be fulfilled either. I felt confused and hurt by the Lord. I had to get really honest with him about my brewing resentment and his seeming lack of care for me. It honestly felt as if he forgot about this desire in my heart and was happy for me to continue doing good work in the kingdom.

If I'm going to wrestle with God, I had better come prepared: tissues, coffee, Bible, journal, and let's not forget a "foot bubbler." Yes, that's right—a device that warms a tub of water for your feet, produces bubbles, and emulates a spa-like atmosphere. The ugly cry and angry words seemed to flow more freely with these simple comforts. And yes, plenty of emotions and questions were hurled toward God that day.

Why was I watching everyone live out the yes I thought was for me?

Did God not care? Did he see me?

What was I doing wrong? Worse yet, was there something fundamentally wrong with me?

God reassured me of his love in some quiet moments after my outbursts. Familiar passages of him knowing the depths of my heart came to mind (Psalm 139). He brought to mind Romans 8 and the groans of creation that come with waiting for redemption.

The Lord helped me remember all the ways he had shown love to me over the years. And in the quiet, with a more settled heart, I sensed another invitation from God. Would I allow him to recalibrate my yes?

Maybe.

Recalibrating didn't mean this yes wouldn't happen, but it might look different from what I'd planned. Again, God challenged me to trust his goodness and faithfulness.

Mark 10:46-52 anchored my heart while I navigated the rough seas of recalibration. It's a story of a blind beggar, Bartimaeus, who is desperate for healing. As Jesus and his disciples journey to Jerusalem, a large crowd follows them. In the midst of the crowd, Bartimaeus yells several times for Jesus to have mercy on him. Jesus hears his cries, and then asks a question: "What do you want me to do for you?"

Really, Jesus? This guy is a blind beggar on the side of the road yelling for you to have mercy on him, and you don't know what he wants?

What does Jesus' question to Bartimaeus stir up for you?

This is where Jesus got ahold of me. It was one of those moments where the Bible read me instead of me reading the Bible. I pondered this moment as I put myself in Bartimaeus's shoes: He's desperate for healing. He shouts out to Jesus. He doesn't care how crazy he looks. He even throws down his coat, likely his only possession, in order to make his way toward Jesus.

I, too, was desperate for God to answer my prayer for motherhood. Did I have a coat that needed to be released from my grip so I could embrace more of Christ's love? Perhaps this recalibrated yes would require letting go of a preconceived notion of what being a mother looked like.

Jesus knows there is power in naming our desires and bringing them before his throne. The words give concreteness to hope and open us up to God's creative possibilities for an answer. I believe this question also gets to a deeper layer underneath the presenting desire. We may want things we didn't know existed.

Bartimaeus requests the obvious, "I want to see!"

"And Jesus says to him, 'Go, for your faith has healed you.' Instantly the man can see, and he follows Jesus down the road."

Bartimaeus receives his physical sight, *and* he receives spiritual sight. He now has the joy of following Jesus. He likely didn't know he needed this spiritual sight as much as his physical sight. He had been a beggar, likely with few friends and little purpose. This beggar now belongs to Jesus' crew and follows him to Jerusalem, which happens to be the most difficult part of the journey. Bartimaeus will be part of seeing Jesus to his death and does not hesitate to go there with him.

I wanted to be a mom, and God revealed to me that underneath this desire a greater desire lived. I enjoyed nurturing others, creating a safe and hospitable environment for people, and helping others grow with Christ. This is what I would do as a mom for biological children, and it's what I did with people in my current circumstances.

God invited me to recalibrate my yes, and in so doing, he wanted to broaden my vision for this yes. The deeper desires of my heart revealed that I could live out "mother" values in a different way. God has given me teams of people to lead and do meaningful work alongside. Partnering and supporting them in any way I can is a way to expand my yes. God has also given me beautiful nieces, friends' children to whom I am a local auntie, and many people I spiritually nurture. God invited me to recalibrate my view of motherhood in order to love and grow those he'd already put in my path.

If recalibrated, how could your yes be expanded?

Frankly, as I received this recalibrated yes, I grieved a great deal. Letting go of dreams is gut wrenching. Releasing expectations embedded in these dreams is painful. I painted a picture in my head of what motherhood should look like, one that my culture encouraged to be true and right. As it turned out, culture may not have the corner market on dreams, or motherhood for that matter.

I learned to trust God and love him, even if my yes looked different. I learned to see the beauty in the different and the faithfulness of the God who gave it to me. I appreciated the opportunities to press into my mother's heart and even saw how God could use this form of motherhood in exponential ways. This became clear when I received a text message, on a difficult Mother's Day, from one of the alumni of my college ministry. The message read: "Happy Mother's Day! You have been such a spiritual momma to me. I am forever thankful for your investment in my life!"

Perhaps God gave me the gift to be a mother to hundreds of people in my lifetime because he knew how much I longed to be mama. Maybe God wasn't holding out, and he actually is generous!

On this side of heaven there will always be a longing unfilled. We won't have total contentment until we reach heaven and enter our glorified state (Romans 8:23). So in the meantime, my heart still aches for the children I never knew. Tears may flow from time to time. And I choose to embrace the recalibrated yes, that I may also experience the joy Jesus has put before me.

SPIRITUAL EXPERIMENT

Spend time in listening prayer. Ask God to reveal ways in which it's difficult to trust him in a yes. What may be the reasons for this? What does he want to say to you? Pay attention to some of the first things that come to mind.

- Are there Scriptures, images, or phrases that come to mind? Write these down and reflect on them.
- Do these reflections align with Scripture? Ask trusted others if this resonates with their understanding of you.
- What are you hearing from God in this?

Chapter Seven

· ·

WAS YES
A MISTAKE?

his yes is not turning out the way I thought it would; in fact, it's a disaster. Sound familiar?

Dave, Mike, and Tim can relate. In 2006 these good friends decided to launch their own health and fitness business. The dream started to form on the golf course when Dave and Mike talked about the new adventure. A friend they played with that day shared about how great his health and fitness business was and that they should think about investing in their own.

Dave and Mike kicked around several ideas, and the thought of helping people get healthier while having a good time doing it sounded appealing. Dave and Mike both valued this in their lives, and they had a third friend, Tim, who held a passion for it too. In fact, Tim had the ability to give much more time to this new business if it actually launched. This seemed perfect. Dave and Mike could keep their full-time jobs, and Tim could run the day-to-day operations.

The friends continued to discern, knowing this was a big yes to commit to. They diligently researched the trends of consumers, the real estate development in the business's location, and the financial forecast for such an investment. Few businesses existed like theirs, and it seemed as if there was a demand for their service in this market.

Long conference calls that went into the wee hours of the morning became a part of their weekly routine. They asked for expert opinions, family and loved ones gave honest thoughts, and they spent time asking God on their own . . . should we do this? All signs pointed to yes, and the partners felt confident God was opening doors to make this dream a reality.

The partners launched their business and it grew. The community buzzed with excitement over this new business that had opened in their neighborhood. Dave, Mike, and Tim also loved using their skills as leaders and entrepreneurs. They ran their business with the highest of standards and ethics, and they desired to honor God and people in all they did. Customers felt cared for when they came through their doors.

Then 2008 happened and the economy crashed. People started looking at their budgets, and discretionary items didn't make the cut. This included health and fitness goals. Their clients slowly dropped off, and it was hard to maintain the ones they had. Additionally, more competitors came on the scene, and larger corporate brands began to appear.

To make matters worse, their office space had a graduated lease, raising the rent each year with the assumption that the business would grow. No one could have predicted the recession. The increased rent became yet another sticking point in an already tense situation. The property managers refused to work with the partners, leaving them wondering how they would make ends meet.

And to top it all off, a dishonest employee stole money from the business and customers. He disappeared from the city, leaving a big mess behind him. Dave, Mike, and Tim's yes became packaged in frustration, disappointment, and confusion. What was God doing?

The partners continued to fight for the yes they believed God had led them to. They desired to care for their customers and their families. They invested resources, time, and a lot of prayer into helping their yes stay afloat.

Finally, after six years of tireless effort, the partners made the painful decision to close the business, and Dave, Mike, and Tim watched their dream die. Had they made a mistake by investing so much in this yes?

What yes have you considered a mistake?

Why is it that when we experience turbulence in our plan, many of us equate it with failure or think we have done something wrong? When saying yes doesn't pan out the way we thought it would, it can lead us to believe that perhaps we misunderstood God, picked the wrong path, or maybe never really heard from him in the first place.

It can be a confusing and frustrating place, which often requires a wrestling of sorts with the Lord. Wrestling with him because it's hard to accept that our picture of what yes was meant to look like is different from what the Lord had in mind, or perhaps allowed. We wrestle with the whys and the what-ifs. In some of our most honest moments, we might wonder if God is really looking out for our good. Why would he let us go down this path, only for it to turn out so badly?

An important question to ask yourself at this point is, Was yes a part of the winding path that is shaping your character and relationship with God?

It takes resilience to weather these storms, and some of them are longer and more painful than we'd like. Dave, Mike, and Tim incurred a lot of loss in their business venture. While those scars are still real, and in many ways continue to heal, they have seen God's faithfulness and provision too. There is a character piece that grew in this time. They learned to rely on the Lord as their resources diminished. They realized the true value of friendship, which weathers such storms and comes out even stronger.

And they took a risk, with each other and with God in this messy yes. As Dave's wife wisely said to them, "You had to try and see what happened, otherwise you would have regretted it for the rest of your life." God cheers on our trying and taking a risk. He is with us as we step out and see what happens with our investment.

In the event that it doesn't work and there is no plan B, perhaps it's well enough to rest in the fact that he is faithful to us in all circumstances. We know that we are deeply loved children of his. We learn resilience through any circumstance with his guidance and care. We find that our confidence and hope is in the King of kings, the Lord of lords, and nothing else.

HOLDING FAITH IN THE MESS

He didn't want his son to die. All he wanted was for his boy to be healthy and have a chance to grow up. The royal official's son was on the brink of death, and the official likely had tried everything to save him. None of his power and money could heal his boy. His boss, King Herod, couldn't heal him. Medicines and doctors hadn't helped either. But there was this man named Jesus who'd turned water into wine at a wedding reception. The Jewish people speculated that he could be the Messiah. It wasn't a secret that the Jews despised King Herod, so what were the chances this Jesus person would help one of his officials? There weren't many options left.

Determined to do what he could for his boy, the royal official embarked on the twenty-mile walk from his home in Capernaum to Cana in Galilee. Rumor had it that Jesus would be making his way through town, the same town where he'd performed the miracle of turning water into wine. Maybe he would perform another miracle for his son.

Uncertainty weaves through this story found in John 4:46-54. As I read it, I imagine myself in the royal official's shoes. I wonder if any of these thoughts rolled through his mind:

What if this doesn't work?

What will the guys back at the king's office think of me when they find out I chased down the local prophet?

It was a long walk to Cana, perhaps as much as eight or ten hours, plenty of time to contemplate one's dire circumstances and the possible outcomes of this risky venture. The royal official's first step toward yes was fueled by desperation.

He finally arrived in Cana that afternoon and the Scripture says, "He went and begged Jesus to come to Capernaum to heal his son, who was about to die." The royal official had never needed to beg anyone to do anything. He held such authority in the king's court that he was on the receiving end of people's pleas. This crisis stripped him of the control he'd become accustomed to. He needed Jesus' help.

Jesus had to know how desperate this man was and that his son meant everything to him. Jesus was more than capable of performing this miracle, and he's compassionate toward the brokenhearted. We read earlier in John 4 of his empathic interactions with the Samaritan woman, which transformed her and her whole village. So what came next from Jesus is surprising.

"Jesus asked, 'Will you never believe in me unless you see miraculous signs and wonders?'"

Yikes. Initially, this seems a bit harsh to me. But as we saw earlier with Jesus and Bartimaeus in Mark 10, the questions Jesus asks draw out a deeper resolve from the people he interacts with. Jesus knows the hidden issues in our souls that need to be addressed, even before we are aware of them. Jesus understood the royal official was searching for a yes to heal his son. Jesus wanted him to find a greater yes, going beyond the miracle. He wanted the official, and the crowd who witnessed this, to shift their worship from the miracles Jesus performed to Jesus himself.

Each time I read this passage, I relate with the royal official and feel the sting of conviction too. In the midst of the messiness of life, I pray for Jesus to show up and change my circumstances. I want him to heal the wrongs and pains in life. This isn't bad, and Jesus tells us to run to him with these things. The question is, Do I need miracles to believe in Jesus, or will I have faith in him regardless of the outcome? Our attempts to find a yes in the miracle will cause us to miss the eternally satisfying yes in Christ.

The royal official was not deterred by Jesus' question, and his fortitude was greater. He took another step toward his yes by pleading again, "Lord, please come now before my little boy dies."

"Then Jesus told him, 'Go back home, your son will live!' And the man believed what Jesus said and started home."

Notice that Jesus didn't do as the official asked. He stayed in Cana and told the official to go back home. Jesus claimed he would find his son alive. This was the first miracle Jesus performed from a distance. Could this really work?

The official's plans for this yes took more twists than expected. I suspect that for a man who was used to making things happen, this was a stretching act of faith. He chose to believe Jesus on his long walk home, or as the NIV translation states, he "took Jesus at his word." He likely stopped and spent the night somewhere, as he would not have arrived home by sunset. I wonder what that night was like? Did he find comfort in Jesus' words as he attempted to sleep? Did he wrestle with doubt and wonder whether his son was dead? If he was anything like me, he may have vacillated between both. The only thing he had to cling to was the word of Jesus, "Your son will live."

How might Jesus be asking you to take him at his word?

If you are in the midst of a turbulent yes, you have more words to cling to than the royal official had; you have the Bible. Some of my go-to verses that help me remember God's faithfulness (particularly in the middle of the night) are the following:

> This is my command—be strong and courageous! Do not be afraid or discouraged. For the LORD your God is with you wherever you go. (Joshua 1:9)

> Yet I still dare to hope
>   when I remember this:
> The faithful love of the LORD never ends!
>   His mercies never cease.
> Great is his faithfulness;
>   his mercies begin afresh each morning.
> I say to myself, "The LORD is my inheritance;
>   therefore, I will hope in him!" (Lamentations 3:21-24)

I am convinced that nothing can ever separate us from God's love. Neither death nor life, neither angels nor demons, neither our fears for today nor our worries about tomorrow—not even the powers of hell can separate us from God's love. No power in the sky above or in the earth below—indeed, nothing in all creation will ever be able to separate us from the love of God that is revealed in Christ Jesus our Lord. (Romans 8:38-39)

As the official neared home, his servants met him with the astonishing news of his son's healing. His fever had suddenly disappeared at the exact time Jesus spoke the words in Cana. Jesus kept his word. Realizing Christ's power and faithfulness led the royal official and his entire household to find their ultimate yes, a yes to believe in Jesus and trust their lives to him.

Through the adversity, the royal official grew his yes with Jesus. He found faith in the Healer, not just the healing. When our yes doesn't turn out the way we thought, might we continue to follow the God who always keeps his word and gives us much grace along the way.

A NEW YES IS BORN

Perhaps your goals don't match what God wanted you to accomplish in this yes. Maybe God could use this detour to bring about a different yes . . . a different dream? When our plan goes sideways, we have an opportunity to trust God to be our guide and our stability. We can practice living a life of openness to Christ by embracing the yes he would have for us . . . even if that yes looks very different.

I always wanted to be a teacher. From the time I was a little girl, I surrounded myself with children and enjoyed helping others learn. When I was eight years old, I was determined to teach my little brother to count to twenty, know his ABCs, and maybe even get him to read. Did I mention he was only three years of age? My high standards followed me into college. I studied diligently and my professors recognized my hard work and passion for education. I wanted to make a difference in our world by investing in young children. I loved watching the light bulb go on in a child's mind when she finally understood a concept and seeing the confidence she gained as a result. This was my life yes, my calling. I knew it was meant to be.

In my senior year at Butler University I received a job offer to teach fifth grade in Indianapolis. Most job offers came in the summer months, so to receive this even before I graduated from college was yet another confirmation in my yes to teach. I spent countless hours preparing my classroom and praying for my future students. I couldn't wait to see how God would work in all our lives that school year.

In mid-August, the first day of school came, and then the first day of school went. As the last child left my classroom, I melted into my chair. All I could think in that moment was, *That did not go well!* I hadn't anticipated that many children. I hadn't foreseen classroom management to be that difficult. I hadn't realized how much love those kiddos would need or how limited I would be to give it. Reality hit me hard that day. I cried, and then cried some more. Wailing might be a more appropriate term for what I did that night. This was not turning out the way I'd thought it would. I wasn't sure I could make it to Labor Day, let alone the end of the school year. Maybe this yes to teaching was a mistake. I felt like my dream crashed down around me. What was God doing?

Panic began to strike my heart as I thought of all the time invested into this yes, all the prayers and hard work. The resources poured into my education were reeling through my mind. What would my professors think? What would my parents say? I was embarrassed to admit this yes may have been a mistake.

LOOKING TO OUR OWN LIVES

In those moments when I feel like everything is falling apart, I am helped by reviewing the hard times in my own past experiences and recalling how they really turned out.

I wasn't a fabulous fifth grade teacher. I certainly didn't love it the way I thought I would. I would be lying to say I accepted my new reality with grace and humility. I didn't. I had a hard time opening up my fists to God and allowing him to show me a new dream. I wanted this yes in teaching to work. I spent two years persevering in this yes of teaching. I found it difficult to hear God because of my own barriers of shame and guilt. I felt bad for getting this wrong. I felt terrible that I'd wasted so many resources pursuing what I thought was my dream job. This path wasn't turning out the way I had thought, not to mention that I questioned my listening skills with God as I thought he'd clearly guided me to this career. Or maybe I listened well but needed a broader vision.

When I hit these places of frustration, and even despair, I find it helpful to "get on the balcony" of my life. This is a popular leadership exercise that helps us gain a bigger vision of what is happening, particularly when we are stuck and can't see the forest for the trees. Getting on the proverbial balcony gives us a new perspective on a situation. For instance, if I'm sitting in my front yard, I get a good look at the things right in front of me. I might notice all the leaves that need to be raked and that we haven't watered the grass lately. When I go to the upstairs bedroom and look out the window, I see a breathtaking display of trees adorned with autumn colors. And everybody else's lawn looks pretty dry, so we must need some rain. It's the same location with two different perspectives.

When I get on the balcony in my personal life, I settle myself in a quiet space, centering on God's presence, and ask for him to show me a different perspective. Psalm 121:1-2 reminds me to do this as the psalmist writes, "I lift up my eyes to the mountains—where does my help come from? My help comes from the LORD, the Maker of heaven and earth" (NIV).

- **Balcony View:** I ask the Lord to get me on the balcony and help me see the bigger picture of what he is doing in my life. Sometimes it's more in the form of begging than politely asking. I ask myself once again, *Am I open to God? Open to seeing and open to hearing?* If I'm not, I need to stay in this space and be honest about what is holding me back from this openness. Some wrestling may be required here, and God is more than able and willing to go there with me. However, if I am open, I proceed to the next step.

- **Reflection:** I reflect back on the messy situation and ask the Lord to reveal his presence in the difficulty. If God is present all the time, it stands to reason that he doesn't leave in the midst of the chaos. And if I truly believe that God is a redemptive God, that he is good, and he loves me, then I have to ask the question, What good is coming out of this? What may I learn from this?

- **Listening:** I may hear answers quickly from the Holy Spirit in the form of images, Scriptures, nudgings, or even an audible voice. Or I may need to reflect back on when I have felt these messy feelings before. When have I thought I failed and God actually was using the circumstance to do something different? Remembering God's faithfulness in the past builds my confidence and assurance that he continues to be redemptive in the present situation.

- **Written Prayers:** Writing down my prayers and reflections with God can be a helpful discipline as I attempt to get on the balcony. It helps me to see patterns in my writing that reveal what God wants me to see. Furthermore, if I continue to keep a record of my written prayers through journaling, it becomes easier to look back on these entries from the past and remember God's faithfulness.

- **Trusted Friends:** There are many times, too, that I need trusted friends to help me see God's faithfulness and how he has carried me in the past. I am grateful for those in my life who graciously, and honestly, helped me to the balcony, especially when it was too hard for me to do on my own.

As I struggled with my own messy yes in teaching, God settled my heart and placed me on the balcony. Through this important process of reflection, prayer, and vulnerability with friends, he brought healing to my shame and doubt. He also delivered a new perspective on my two years of teaching.

Where do you see God's faithfulness in your circumstances?

He gave me insight into the ways I learned to persevere and find joy, even when my circumstances challenged me. He revealed how I learned to teach in creative ways, and that I cherished the times I could invest deeply in my students. During this season of teaching, God gave me opportunities to volunteer with a campus ministry I loved, which gave me vision for how to use my teaching skills in a different way and on a different path. God used my time in teaching to help prepare me for a particular kind of teaching, a teaching of the gospel to college students, which I have now been doing for the last twenty years and find great joy in. Teaching fifth grade wasn't a mistake, it was a necessary step toward a greater yes God had for me.

MAKING OUR OWN MESS

God is merciful with us and he does guide and shape our character while we say yes. It's important to remember that we are not perfect people, and "we all fall short of God's glorious standard" (Romans 3:23). Sometimes we make decisions that are more out of our brokenness than a desire to follow Jesus. For instance, you could decide to be a listening friend for people, which can be seen as helpful and empathic. But the underlying motivation is to ensure you are always the one listening and giving advice and never the one who is vulnerable and needing help. The listening becomes a self-serving, protective mechanism.

Sometimes we end up saying yes to things that are not in line with God's heart and Word or might be motivated from our own selfish desires. We contribute to our own messy yeses at times and don't even realize it. For example, you could say yes to a promotion at work that would double your pay and give you future advancement. However, it is known that a certain amount of bending the truth will be needed in order to make the numbers work and satisfy the customers. Everyone does this, so it shouldn't be a big deal. The yes suddenly and eventually becomes a hindrance in your relationship with God and honoring him.

If we are unfamiliar with God's Word and his character, we can be led in a direction that is more anchored in the world than in the truth and hope of Christ. Our yeses change as our understanding of God increases. The more we understand God's heart and dig into the Scriptures, the more we can say yes with greater clarity and wisdom. We can have a better framework for what will give honor to God, and we can receive confidence and freedom as we follow our yes and our Lord.

Additionally, we may need to spend time getting to know ourselves on a deeper level. As we learn more about our own shadow sides and who we truly are in Christ, we can discern more clearly what might be influencing a yes. Remember that Jesus loves to bring healing and wholeness to us. He is all about bringing us back to our true selves in Christ, who we were created to be. As we walk with Jesus, and in the company of trusted friends, we learn more about who we are and who we are meant to be. And sometimes our journey to yes brings this discovery about all the more.

Getting to yes rarely follows a straight path. It can be turbulent, uncomfortable, and nerve wracking. It can be messy. Getting to yes will require courage and a good measure of faith in our great and sovereign God. As we encounter unexpected detours on our journey, God may surprise us with joy and reveal our purpose as we follow him.

> *Getting to yes rarely follows a straight path.*

SPIRITUAL EXPERIMENT

Take a risk in trying something new. It could be starting conversation with a stranger or volunteering in your community. Or something else.

What went well? What didn't go as planned? Spend time asking God to reveal what he wants you to know about him and about yourself as a result.

Chapter Eight

· ·

THE PAIN
OF YES

When he was only two years old, Jerald Cosey's parents died. His grandparents stepped into the gap and raised him. He understood at an early age the value of learning from his elders and how to relate to them.

Jerald grew up, graduated from Kentucky State, and landed a sought-after job in pharmaceutical sales. He married his college sweetheart, and they had three beautiful children. All seemed to go according to plan.

Jerald won top sales awards and enjoyed much success in his company. Then his company downsized, and after thirteen years of employment, he lost his job. Jerald knew this happened frequently in the industry, but he had not planned on it happening to him.

What would he do now?

He met with his pastor who encouraged him to take a moment and reflect. His pastor asked a question similar to the one referenced earlier, in chapter six, between Jesus and Bartimaeus: *What do you want?*

In recent years, Jerald had discovered there were epidemic numbers of senior citizens who experienced isolation in nursing homes. This broke his heart. As Jerald faced this time between jobs, he began to wonder how God might use his friendships with the elderly to bring blessing to this community. He began weekly visits to a local nursing home and developed friendships with the residents there. These weeks turned into months and eventually years. Jerald visited one gentleman every week for five years. This not only served his elderly friend, it also blessed Jerald. He thoroughly enjoyed his time at the nursing home and invited others to join him in this yes he had committed to God. Eventually, from this effort, a ministry called Graceful Moments was born. The mission statement reads, "We are children of God, serving Christ by serving the senior citizens of our world. We are dedicated to minimizing isolation, one graceful moment at a time."

Jerald did land another job in pharmaceutical sales and continued to run Graceful Moments. In the meantime, Jerald developed an illness that, over the course of five years, took a toll on his body. He eventually became incredibly ill and was hospitalized for several weeks. Again, this was not the plan he'd imagined for nearing middle age: battling a life-threatening illness. Why was this happening?

When pain hits, the *why* question is natural. We want to make sense of things. "If this happens, then this should happen." For example, "If I do good deeds, then God should bless me." And by "bless" I mean, "give me what I want." Nowhere in Scripture does it say that if you follow Christ, you will live a pain-free life. In fact, the pain may get worse as you go against the grain of culture and irritate the enemy, a.k.a. the devil.

Our tendency is to blame someone when we are in pain. It's important to remember that the Lord doesn't necessarily cause the pain. We live in a broken world with broken systems and broken bodies. God works within this brokenness and is able to redeem pain and help us grow through it.

We may never know why something has happened. It's not a helpful question to ponder for too long, as God's thoughts and ways are too complex and mysterious for us to understand. A better question to ask is, "What now, God?"

This is the question Jerald held as he lay in the hospital bed. He trusted Christ in his life and knew the Lord was up to something, even in the midst of the pain. Eventually, Jerald healed, and he paid attention to the immense gratitude he had for the nurses who cared for him during his illness. This esteem for healthcare professionals, coupled with his heart for the elderly, led Jerald to make his volunteer ministry with the elderly into a full-time career. After much prayer, he left eighteen years of employment in pharmaceutical sales. Jerald accepted a job with the nursing home he volunteered with and received a 40 percent pay cut. He trusted God with the cost of this yes and moved forward with excitement.

How might the question, What now, God? shift your perspective?

Several years into the journey of the new job, challenges arose. Operating a nursing home took enormous amounts of emotional, spiritual, and physical energy. He felt drained. Jerald noticed he was not alone in this feeling. Ironically, caretakers can feel so depleted that they don't have energy to connect with anyone else. As a result, they become just as isolated as the people they are tending to.

Jerald had not expected the pain of this yes to be so great and began to wonder if he'd made a mistake. He held the pain while he held on to Christ and asked the question, "What now?"

The familiar question, What do you want? helped guide Jerald once again. He loved speaking, teaching, and having a positive influence on others. Jerald began to wonder if God would use this pain of burnout to propel him to speak words of healing and hope to the healthcare community.

Jerald decided to say yes to motivational speaking. Perhaps this could be a way to earn a supplemental income and bring good news to people. If healthcare facilities increased connection with their employees as well as their patients, then isolation and burnout could be minimized. He incorporated his life story along with the bright moments and painful experiences. God used all of it.

Jerald's yes to speaking grew, and the executives at the nursing home took notice. They promoted him to his current position, director of operational leadership development. This role allows him to empower leaders in ninety facilities across the Midwest as well as speak to healthcare professionals across the country.

Jerald reflected on the importance of continuing relationships with seniors in his life. "It is truly a mutual blessing. These elders mentor me while I meet with them. Who would have thought that two senior White women from Kentucky and Indiana would mentor a middle-aged Black man? It has been a very unifying experience and refuels me emotionally. I love it."

Some yeses are filled with the painful question of why. In God's grace, we journey to the what that we truly want and find healing for our souls, and help others find healing too.

PAIN AND LIES

"Don't believe the lie!" exclaimed Reverend Brenda Salter McNeil.

On this balmy January day in 2002, twelve hundred Inter-Varsity staff gathered in Orlando, Florida, for our national staff conference with InterVarsity Christian Fellowship. We were supposed to hear from our National Director of Black Campus Ministry, Alex Anderson. But two days before the conference, the unthinkable happened and Alex died of a massive heart attack. Dead at age forty-seven, he left behind a wife and children.

Although I didn't know Alex personally, I grieved with my colleagues. Bewilderment and confusion hung in the air. Why would God allow this to happen to a man like Alex? He dedicated his life to racial justice and reconciliation, loved students, and empowered Black students to lead courageously with Jesus.

Our national leaders asked Dr. Brenda to speak in Alex's place. She had been a campus minister with InterVarsity. She knew us and we knew her. And Dr. Brenda, filled by the Spirit, didn't mince words when it came to telling the truth. She shouted from the pulpit that morning, "Don't believe the lie!" That phrase seared in my memory.

Dr. Brenda shared stories of Black leaders in the not so distant past who gave their lives, quite literally, for the advancement of the gospel and reconciliation between races. She noted the pattern of people dying tragically as they led in this area and that it could be easy to believe the enemy's lie, which she stated: "If you step into this kingdom work, you will be destroyed."

Dr. Brenda unpacked the fear behind this lie and that fear does not come from Jesus, as I recall. The devil would like nothing more than to keep us bound up in fear so that we will never say yes to the work of peace and wholeness in Christ. We may enter pain as we say yes to important kingdom work, but that pain will not be in vain. Christ will be with us, even in physical death, as we will have his presence eternally. And who is to say there will always be an outcome of physical death and tragedy? By believing in this fear-based lie, we limit God to our own conclusions.

I resonated deeply with Dr. Brenda's words. I sat in my seat that morning with tears trickling down my face. Why was I crying? I wasn't on the front lines of racial justice, although I was learning much in this season. As I waded through the tears, I discovered that my heart bought into a variation of this lie.

If you continue to grow as a ministry leader, you will never get married.

I was embarrassed to admit this lie, and it gripped my heart in fear. I knew it was not nearly as painful as death, and it seemed small compared to the heroic efforts of those working for racial reconciliation. But at that moment, in my world and in my soul, this lie felt incredibly painful. Most of my friends in ministry were married at this time of life and choosing one of two paths: they either reduced their hours to begin their families or left ministry altogether. In 2002, I did not see many examples of married women with children who held leadership positions.

A reality in my Midwest neck of the woods was that there seemed to be more social and theological acceptance around men in ministry leadership than women. I had both men and women tell me that my combination of yeses was too intimidating for most men.

The pain of loneliness and longing overtook my convictions, and I began to doubt my choices. My circumstances and surrounding voices nailed down a deeper lie that I had harbored for years: *you are too much. I need to tone down my voice, leadership, and personality to be accepted by people.*

I began to believe I would need to say no to future leadership positions and stop maturing as a disciple of Jesus if I had any hope of marrying. When I say this out loud, it seems ridiculous, and it is. Of course, Jesus would want me to keep growing and maturing in his ways. However, when the lie becomes so loud inside your heart, it becomes hard to hear the whispers of truth.

As more promotions were offered, I continued to wrestle with God. I said yes to leading, but fear still hovered near my heart. I tried to tone down my personality as I dated men, but I wasn't very successful. I slowly began to move (maybe crawl) from the question of Why is God taking me down this path? to What does God want me to learn? I should be happy to gain more influence, not scared that my dreams of marriage were moving further away from me. It certainly didn't feel right to pretend to be someone I wasn't.

I received healing for my mind and heart as I took in the truth of who I was in Christ. It gave me abundance in life, not limitations. Christ affirmed the good gifts he chose to give me, not least of which is leadership, and that I am wonderfully enough in him.

A special thanks to the plethora of therapists I've enlisted over the years who have helped me be open to receiving such truths!

What truth from God do you need to hear?

I began to embrace the life God gave me. Go Big or Go Home became my mantra. I committed to grow as deep and wide as I could in Jesus and say yes to opportunities that stretched my leadership all the more. I said yes to Jesus' invitation to unashamedly bring my whole self to the table. I determined that God's presence would go with me, and I would just need to trust God for the longings of my heart. I knew this would still mean pain. I continued to live within the realities of my geography and culture. But the manner in which I navigated those realities would shift. The empowered love of Jesus seemed a better route than a limiting fear of people and self.

God used my pain of being a single woman in leadership to bring my attention to a deep-seated lie that did not serve me. I may not have experienced this freedom in my soul without the wrenching pain. And although I'm now married, and God delivered what I thought was an impossible gift of marriage, the pain of leadership is still present. Leadership comes with a cost no matter how you slice it. It simply takes different shapes in different seasons, and it always drives me back to the feet of Jesus.

THE POWER IN THE PAIN

"My soul is crushed with grief to the point of death" (Matthew 26:38).

Jesus uttered these words in the Garden of Gethsemane just before the soldiers came to arrest him. No one understands pain better than Jesus. Pain played a principal role in his mission, and in our salvation.

Jesus' journey to the cross was one painful experience after another.

John 13 tells of Jesus' Last Supper with his disciples on the day before his crucifixion. He modeled servant leadership by washing their feet, a lowly job on earth but of high value in the kingdom of heaven. He knew the end was coming, and he knew it was going to be a brutal death. Instead of focusing on his own comfort or fear, he chose to wash their dirty, disgusting feet on this night. By doing this, Jesus communicated to his disciples the priority to lead others selflessly and sacrificially. It is intriguing that this is how Jesus chose to spend his last hours alive.

Jesus went a step further and washed everyone's feet, *including his disciple Judas Iscariot.* Jesus knew Judas had already betrayed him by going to the leading priests and temple guards. These religious authorities plotted to kill Jesus as he continued to gain more influence with the people and threatened their positions of power. It must have been painful for Jesus to know Judas had gone behind his back and planned to destroy him. Judas was one of his cadre of twelve men that he had poured three years of life and friendship into. And yet he humbly washed Judas's feet, modeling for all of us how to love those who betray us.

Jesus' selfless love propelled him to keep moving toward the cross. John 17 records the prayer of Jesus to God the Father on this final evening. The prayer reveals his love for us and his deep desire that we would reflect this love for others:

I have given them the glory you gave me, so they may be one as we are one. I am in them and you are in me. May they experience such perfect unity that the world will know that you sent me and that you love them as much as you love me. Father, I want these whom you have given me to be with me where I am. Then they can see all the glory you gave me because you loved me even before the world began! (John 17:22-24)

Jesus desperately wants people to experience perfect love and unity, which can only come through knowing God the Father. We struggle with love and unity. Much of the pain in our own lives and in the world stems from a lack of love and unity. When we are connected to God, we are joined to this deep well of love and unity that never goes dry and always satisfies. God created us and the entire universe with the intention of shalom. *Shalom* is a Hebrew word, rich in meaning, that was used in original translations of Scripture. It succinctly means peace and wholeness that allows all creation to flourish. Everyone and everything is rooted in God's harmony and love. Sign me up for that, please!

But here's the problem: as humans, we've bumped God out of the driver's seat and decided that we can steer the car more effectively on our own. Inevitably, we get into a fender bender with someone or even total the car. Accidents happen. To be clear, somewhere and at some time we all mess up and have been messed with by others. Shalom is broken. It's painful. Selfishness, pride, deceit, anger, and a litany of other actions are expressions of this brokenness. Romans 3:23 says, "For everyone has sinned; we all fall short of God's glorious standard." No one gets a pass on this.

Our individual sin has had an effect on our world as we experience the brokenness of poverty, hatred, and decay of our planet . . . just to name a few. Simply turn on the nightly news if you don't believe our world is broken and in desperate need of healing. Romans 8:20-22 says,

> Against its will, all creation was subjected to God's curse. But with eager hope, the creation looks forward to the day when it will join God's children in glorious freedom from death and decay. For we know that all creation has been groaning as in the pains of childbirth right up to the present time.

Sin, or brokenness, separates us from God. God's glorious standard is perfectly holy and just. Anything that isn't to this standard cannot coexist in his presence. Our brokenness destroys our relationship with him, and we aren't able to receive his love. God's perfect justice requires a penalty for our sin. There is nothing but pain on this path without God. Romans 6:23 says, "For the wages of sin is death." The consequence for sin is death, separation from God, and we've earned it.

But God does the impossible. The unthinkable.

He chose to pay the penalty for our sin. He heals the brokenness of our world and of our hearts. He offers forgiveness and grace for all the mess. In simplistic terms, God gives us a get out of jail free card. The last half of Romans 6:23 states, "but the free gift of God is eternal life through Christ Jesus our Lord."

The penalty for our sin is paid through the death of Jesus Christ, God's own Son. It's in this ugly, painful, humiliating crucifixion that there is reconciliation between God and all who profess Jesus as Lord of their lives. Perfect love and unity with God are restored and offered to all who believe. We gain freedom from shame, guilt, and sin. We receive a new and redeemed life here on earth as well as for all of eternity. If we choose to receive this free gift, we then work through Jesus to heal the broken places of this world. We journey with Jesus in our yes.

If you have never said yes to surrendering your life to Jesus and trusting him, I urge you to consider that invitation now. It's the most important invitation you'll receive in your lifetime.

Perhaps you have said yes to Jesus, but life has taken a toll, and you've found yourself on a detour. May I ask you to consider a fresh start with Jesus and receive his forgiveness and grace all over again? Our journey with Jesus is not a straight path upward. It has many curves, valleys, and deserts. Jesus longs to do this journey with you.

"Preach the gospel to yourself every day."

In his book *The Discipline of Grace*, Jerry Bridges writes that you should "preach the gospel to yourself every day." It's in the remembering of Jesus' journey to the cross that I remember how much I need his grace and how much I need to extend it to others.

I remember Jesus' prayer in the Garden of Gethsemane. Mark 14:32-42 depicts Jesus anguishing in prayer for himself and for his disciples. He knows the pain that is ahead. He is honest in the pain. He goes to the One he knows will help him through this, God the Father.

Jesus says to the disciples, "My soul is crushed with grief to the point of death." Mark continues to write, "He went on a little farther and fell to the ground. . . . 'Abba, Father,' he cried out, 'everything is possible for you. Please take this cup of suffering away from me. Yet I want your will to be done, not mine.'"

Jesus wanted the will of the Father more than his comfort. God didn't take the pain away. Jesus' pain on the cross would be our path to unity with God. We so badly want our pain taken away. We doubt God is with us if we feel pain. Pain leads us to growth in our journey to yes. It may be the path to knowing Christ's love all the more.

Next, I remember his arrest. The authorities apprehend him because they are threatened by his power and influence (Luke 22). He has committed no crime, and false charges are put upon him. He is flogged, whipped, beaten, and chastised as he moves from one court to the next. All the while, Peter, one of his closest friends and disciples, denies knowing Jesus. Peter denies knowing him not once, not twice, but three times while Jesus is being tortured. The pain continues for Jesus, and now for Peter as he wrestles with his fear and guilt.

I remember Jesus carrying his heavy cross on his bleeding back, all by himself. There are crowds jeering at him. His mother and several other women follow him closely, holding their own pain as they watch in horror (Mark 15).

As Jesus is nailed brutally to the cross, he is still ministering to others.

As Jesus is being nailed brutally to the cross, he is still ministering to others. Jesus says, "Father, forgive them, for they don't know what they are doing," as the people mock and sneer at him (Luke 23:34). He tells the "disciple he loved" (presumably John), to take care of his mother and his mother to take care of John (John 19:26-27).

The thief hanging next to Jesus expresses his belief in Jesus being the Messiah and says, "Jesus, remember me when you come into your Kingdom." Jesus answers him, "I assure you, today you will be with me in paradise" (Luke 23:42-43).

I remember Jesus gasping his last breath on the cross as darkness comes over the whole land. Jesus exclaims, "It is finished," and his physical body dies (John 19:30).

The transaction is complete. He has paid the price of our freedom with his death.

Then I remember the very good news.

There is pain and grief for two days, but on the third day, God does the impossible, again. Jesus conquers death and is raised from the grave. There is an empty tomb! Because Jesus lives eternally, we now may live eternally.

There is an intersection of pain and shalom on this side of heaven. Pain is part of our journey here on earth. It is often an integral part of our journey to yes. But heaven broke through our messed-up world with the life and resurrection of Jesus. So we get a taste of God's shalom here on earth and the hope of healing.

We experience shalom when we witness an act of kindness toward another human being. We savor this shalom in the moments of a beautiful sunset after a chaotic day. We feel this shalom when we use our strengths to build others up. We get closer to shalom as we draw closer to Christ. And one glorious day, either when God calls us home to heaven or upon his return to earth, we will see total and complete shalom once again.

Jesus encountered tremendous pain on his journey to yes. While it had the appearance of failure and defeat, he remained faithful to the end. Death did not win and the story did not end. God used Christ's pain for a purpose. May the pain in our journey to yes usher in great amounts of Christ's love and unity to a world that is in desperate need of this hope. To God be the glory and shalom to all of creation.

SPIRITUAL EXPERIMENT

Listen to Pray as You Go (https://pray-as-you-go.org), an online daily prayer session that gives a framework for praying on your own. Music, Scripture, and reflective questions are used each day to help you connect with God.

. . . .

Chapter Nine

THE CHOICE
TO SAY NO

S hould I stay or should I go? This question plagued Tammy
for several years.

Tammy desired to do meaningful work outside the home. Her
career in college ministry gave her the flexibility she needed in
this season of life, although she began to wonder if her career
might need to be put on hold. These days, it seemed like a full-
time job to anticipate the care needed for aging parents, raise
young children, and give special attention to her one child with
significant health challenges. She'd already cut down her work
hours to accommodate these life circumstances, and still it seemed
like too much.

Saying no to things came easily, and with good reason. Tammy
had to be strategic with her time. She continually wrestled
with the question of whether she should stay
on staff with campus ministry. For all practical reasons, it seemed like her time needed
to end. No one would blame her for saying
no to full-time work, yet she still longed to
make an impact on college campuses.

*What might be good
reasons to consider
a no instead of a
yes right now?*

Tammy prayed and kept being honest with God about the desires of her heart. Her prayer with God was, "I trust you see my heart, even though I don't see possibilities."

Just as resigning from campus ministry seemed inevitable, a new invitation arrived in Tammy's inbox. It was an email inviting her to participate in a women's leadership cohort with her campus ministry. *Are you kidding? No way. This is definitely not the right timing*, Tammy thought. She could barely do her day job, let alone extra leadership tasks.

Her supervisor would never allow this, as she was only working ten hours a week. Why did she get this invitation? This must be a mistake.

Tammy shared the news of the invitation with a trusted mentor who posed the question, "Why don't you just see what the possibilities are before you say no?"

Her prayer reverberated in her soul: "I trust you see my heart, even though I don't see possibilities."

Tammy had honest conversations with her supervisor and me, the director of the project. We affirmed the good gifts Tammy held and acknowledged the obstacles. It seemed to us that Tammy's limited hours were likely for a season, and God might very well be preparing her for something more in the next few years. We were willing to see what God might do in Tammy's life if she said yes to this investment. We committed to find creative ways to support Tammy in this endeavor and trust God for the outcomes.

Our yeses gave Tammy confirmation and confidence to turn her initial no into a yes.

In the next eighteen months of the cohort, God grew Tammy's vision for what was possible in her future. He used the cohort of women to call out gifts in Tammy, and Tammy saw hope for a more agile leadership structure that could accommodate women in the throes of motherhood. At the same time, her children were in a different season of growth and health, which made even more room for Tammy's leadership possibilities.

Two years later, the position of regional director became available in her geographic area. She currently held the associate role and wasn't sure she wanted the host of challenges that came with the full director job. Tammy said a quiet no to herself but noticed her heart restless for a new adventure.

Then, twenty-four hours before the deadline to submit the regional director application, Tammy received an intriguing email from the hiring vice president. The VP reminded her of the urgent due date, and one sentence in particular sent Tammy into another round of prayer: "If you need a little more time to fill out this application, feel free to let me know."

Tammy's quiet no suddenly became a noisy maybe.

Perhaps God wanted to use her leadership gifts of strategy and vision, combined with her context as a Chinese American woman and mother. There were not many examples of people who looked like her in this type of leadership.

Tammy reflected, "I wanted to see what God would do if I said yes."

With a sudden burst of energy, she filled out the application and submitted it. Shortly thereafter, she received the job offer.

But because Tammy said no so often, she wrestled with how to say yes.

If she said yes, it would mean oversight of multiple states, which would mean increased travel and more leadership challenges. Her husband would have to be on board, as it would mean a change in their family's organization.

As Tammy and her husband processed this decision, he encouraged her to say yes, and he would be the one to say no to more leadership.

He recognized that Tammy had said no multiple times as their children were very young, which had enabled him to say yes to many things. He had paved many paths in his own career and achieved much already. If Tammy said yes to this, he would take on more responsibilities with their children, and Tammy would have more time for this opportunity.

Sometimes one person's no gives room for another's yes.

With her husband on board, she now needed a clear yes from God.

Tammy planned a trip with her mom and sister. It was rare to have this sacred space with them. They spent time in Mauritius, an island just off the southern coast of Africa where her mother grew up.

As Tammy enjoyed reconnecting with her family, God reminded her of important parts of her life story. A life map began to form in Tammy's mind.

Tammy remembered her paternal grandmother, Chi Ching, who fled Yunnan, China, during the civil war. Her grandmother packed up four children while pregnant with her fifth and boarded a plane to Nanjing, China, to meet her father. Chi Ching and her children were asked to leave that plane because one of the children was crying too much. They waited until the next day for another plane, and when they arrived in Nanjing, they heard terrible news. The plane they had intended to take ended up crashing and, sadly, no one survived. In this horrible tragedy, God's sovereign hand held this strong woman and her children and gave them a chance for a new life.

Tammy remembered her maternal grandmother, Kihow Moy, who sailed on a boat from southern China to the island of Mauritius in search of a better life. She traveled with her infant son and father-in-law on this month-long voyage. One year later,

Kihow Moy gave birth to Tammy's mother, Ellen, and five more children would follow after that.

Then Tammy remembered her own mother's story, filled with perseverance through obstacles. Ellen was the oldest daughter and desperately wanted to go to college, but she lived a culture where women were expected to find a husband, have children, and not go to college. Even to attend high school, Tammy's mother needed to convince her parents she could handle all the family chores, care for her five siblings, and still keep up with her schoolwork. This meant early mornings and late nights, but she dedicated herself to the tasks.

After graduation, Ellen applied and gained admittance to a one-year secretarial program. Unable to find a job after she completed the program, she applied and was accepted to a nursing school in England. Disappointment lingered, as she was not allowed to attend because girls were meant to stay close to home, not go away to school.

This small, slight woman was tough minded. She eventually found a secretarial job in Mauritius, and after three years she decided it wasn't going to help her career. She applied for a job in Zambia with a private company. Tammy's mother achieved high marks for her work and received praise for being trilingual (Hakka is her family language, French is the language of Mauritius, along with English). She then landed in Kenya, where she gained a job with the United Nations as a secretary. This job allowed her to travel and see the world, which eventually brought her to New York. There Tammy's mom met Tammy's dad, and their own adventure began.

As Tammy traced the life stories of the women in her family, she marveled at the strength God had given them. These women swam against the current of culture, caring for their families and leading courageous lives. Tammy came by her bravery and strength honestly from these women. Additionally, as Tammy reflected on her own life journey, she gained even more clarity on God's work through her yeses in recent years: her yes to the leadership cohort, the yes to partnering well with her husband, and even her original yes to the mission of serving college students all those years ago in college.

This was nearly enough for Tammy to say yes to this regional director role, but God had one more important confirmation to give Tammy.

She listened to a keynote speech given by Sarah Breuel, a missionary in Italy, who challenged an audience at a student mission conference that winter. Sarah Breuel said something that stuck with Tammy: "God is not looking for heroes. He's looking for people who will say yes."

"God is not looking for heroes. He's looking for people who will say yes."

In that moment, Tammy opened her heart to the Lord and sensed him reassuring her with these words: Trust me, I will be with you. Whatever you pictured a regional director to be from your past experiences, you can let go of. There is no measuring up. You don't have to be the hero. You don't need to be a perfect leader or well known. You don't have to be the example for all women, mothers, and staff of color. Be faithful and do what I'm calling you do to. Are you willing to serve my people and lead them well? Will you create a healthy team of people who love me and love the mission?

With God's assurance of this invitation, Tammy had confidence that she could indeed say yes to this new job and that he had prepared her for the task.

There are good reasons to say no and good reasons to say yes. It's in the discernment of these choices we find ourselves drawn near to God and learn more of who we truly are in him.

JONAH—NO AND CLENCHED FISTS

There is a fine line between strong willed and stubborn. I come by both qualities honestly in my German/Norwegian family tree. Strong willed describes a person filled with determination and perseverance even amid adversity. A stubborn person embodies determination and matches it with irrational persistence. I have seen both show up while finding a yes, usually accompanied by either opening a hand to God's plan or shaking a raised fist.

The book of Jonah shares the story of the book's namesake and his stubborn no to God's invitation.

"Get up and go to the great city of Nineveh. Announce my judgment against it because I have seen how wicked its people are" (Jonah 1:2). The Lord commanded the prophet Jonah to complete this task around 750 BC.

The yes God calls us to is not always enjoyable. Nineveh was the capital city in Assyria, and this country had terrorized the Jewish people of Israel for decades through war, murder, theft, and hostile takeovers of their land. But God was on mission and needed a servant to announce his harsh reality to these people so they might have an opportunity to change their ways. The Lord was serious in this call and clearly gave Jonah the plan.

Not one part of Jonah desired to give this warning to his people's enemy. After all, they might heed the warning and repent! Jonah understood God's character, and Jonah knew the Lord would end up forgiving these enemies of his. Jonah couldn't stand the thought of God's mercy and grace extending to the blood-thirsty Assyrians. He began to shake his fist toward God.

So Jonah chose to say no and attempted to escape the Lord. He literally ran in the opposite direction of the yes. Jonah departed Jerusalem and hopped on a boat sailing to Tarshish, which was the city farthest away from Nineveh. His no was firm, and he had a plan for keeping it that way.

Choosing to avoid God tempts many of us. We want to dodge the hard thing and continue to live as we choose. If we say yes to God's path, we may have to deal with our sin or other people's brokenness, and it seems too hard. Deciding to say no to God's path may create comfort for us, but it could result in painful consequences.

It can be challenging to know whether avoidance or wisdom fuels our no. Is it being strong willed or stubborn? Again, creating space to reflect on our motivations alongside God's commands and character is helpful. Stubborn may look like choosing no to stay in a sinful pattern. Or you might find yourself not wanting to talk to God about this decision or process it with anyone else. Your mind is made up and the door is closed.

Jonah experienced some consequences to his no while sailing to Tarshish. A huge storm nearly capsized the ship, and the sailors panicked. They did everything they knew to survive: shouted to their gods for help, threw items overboard to lighten the load, and finally cast lots to ask their gods who the problem was.

Meanwhile, Jonah slept at the bottom of the boat, seemingly unconcerned. He likely knew that this storm was all about him, and he didn't care. The sailors figured out that Jonah was running from his God, and Jonah admitted that this storm likely was the doing of the Lord to get his attention. The best thing the sailors could do was throw him overboard and all would calm down.

I can't help but laugh out loud. He'd rather risk dying in a storm and putting the lives of all these men at risk than say yes to God and give the Assyrians a chance to know him. This is a man committed to his no!

The sailors didn't know what else to do, so they threw Jonah overboard, and all quieted on the boat and in the sea. The infamous great fish then swallowed Jonah up, and he was there for three days. I don't understand how terrifying it would be to live in the belly of whale, nor do I want to find out. Apparently, it scared Jonah enough to open his clenched fist and become slightly more open handed with his no to God. In Jonah 2:1-9 he prayed to God, acknowledged his circumstances, and recognized God's power. Jonah begged for his life and promised to follow God's lead, and the fish spit Jonah out upon the Lord's orders (Jonah 2:10).

I'm not making this stuff up.

Jonah's no became a yes as God gave him a second chance to follow his lead. This is a wonderful reminder of God's grace to us in our journey to yes. As my counselor says, "The Holy Spirit is so committed to you, he will keep bringing something back around until you are ready to receive it." Thank you, Jesus.

Jonah went to Nineveh and said, "Forty days from now Nineveh will be destroyed!" (Jonah 3:4).

This was his inspirational vision cast for a transformed life? The speech was not exactly winsome and compelling. Granted, Jonah obeyed God and shared the message he was asked to share, but he didn't go further to tell much more. I wonder if Jonah's heart was really in it or if he was simply checking off an obedience to-do list. There's no mention of how to repent or any description of God's character. Jonah simply says, "You will be destroyed." Mic drop.

"The people of Nineveh believed God's message, and from the greatest to the least, they declared a fast and put on burlap to show their sorrow" (Jonah 3:5). Miraculously, that's all that was needed in Jonah's yes as the whole city ignited in confession and repentance. The king and his nobles even sent out a decree telling people they needed to mourn for their sins, turn away from their old ways, and pray earnestly to God to have mercy on them.

This is yet another example of how God can use even the smallest amount of faith to accomplish his plan through us. God must have been stirring in the Assyrians' hearts for them to be ready for such a dramatic response.

Did the Lord really need Jonah to get this done? No. The Lord could have done this all on his own without Jonah, but I believe he wanted to work through Jonah to deliver this message. Likely, there was a deeper invitation for Jonah in the midst of this journey.

With little effort on Jonah's part, the Assyrians repented of their ways, and God spared their city. This outcome ticked off Jonah. His fist formed and began to shake again.

> Didn't I say before I left home that you would do this, LORD? That is why I ran away to Tarshish! I knew that you are a merciful and compassionate God, slow to get angry and filled with unfailing love. You are eager to turn back from destroying people. Just kill me now, LORD! I'd rather be dead than alive if what I predicted will not happen. (Jonah 4:2-3)

Ironically, the mercy God gave Jonah through the great fish rescue is the same mercy Jonah has a hard time extending to his enemies. This is likely the deeper invitation God had for the prophet. God wanted Jonah, and all of us, to know that his forgiveness is available to all people, and no one is outside the bounds of God's grace.

It appears that God handpicked Jonah for this role in the story of Nineveh's repentance so he could personally witness God's heart and power. Additionally, this was also Jonah's opportunity to repent of his pride and perhaps even gain freedom from the bonds of hate toward the Assyrians. If he released this hatred, less bitterness and more love would fill Jonah.

Sadly, we don't get the impression that Jonah ever got to this point, at least not by the end of the written story. The book ends with Jonah shaking his raised fist to God saying he was "angry enough to die" (Jonah 4:9). While Jonah technically says yes to God and obeys him, he did it with heels dug into the ground and wanting it on his terms. One hundred twenty thousand people in Nineveh may have sprouted new life, but Jonah's one heart grew a root system of anger. It is possible to say yes and still say no in our souls.

God does not force himself upon us. He loves us and gives us the choice to hold open hands or clenched fists, to be strong willed or stubborn.

How is it possible to say yes and still say no in our souls?

THE CREATIVE NO

My friend Jill is an out-of-the-box thinker and great visionary. About a decade ago, her creativity and inspiration spilled over into my life. "You need to start writing. Get your voice out there. It would be a great way for you to expand your influence and impact others. I'll set up a blog for you to get started."

As Jill spoke these words, they fell on my very skeptical ears. *My voice is just fine right here,* I thought, *in my own head and over a strong cup of coffee with a dear friend.* I wanted no part of blogging or any type of writing, for that matter. It seemed a daunting task, and I had nothing to say that others haven't already said. I didn't have the first clue on how to write for others. *No, I'm not doing this.*

It's not that I opposed writing. I enjoyed creative writing as a student. Since college, I've written my prayers in journals as a way of communicating to God. But I'm not a writer. A writer is creative, eloquent, and thoughtful. I'm a counselor, teacher, and campus minister. I'll stay in my lane, thank you.

Jill didn't take no for an answer. She believed that my story of finding hope in Christ and all the life lessons I'd gathered along the way would be an encouragement to people. I thought Jill was a loyal friend and a bit biased.

Jill convinced me to start small in this adventure and assured me I could use the blog site as space to practice writing and see if I enjoyed it. Jill tried to cheer me on in this very hesitant yes. Did I mention that she is persuasive? She set up my site, encouraged me to go for it, and off I went.

I blogged a total of three times in six months.

Feelings of inadequacy, paired with the busyness of life, made my no stronger than my yes.

Unbeknown to me, this seed for writing found its way into my soul. Nearly a year later, I attended a women's conference, and the speaker challenged us to ask God if there was something we needed to stop putting off and just do. I had nothing come to mind. I didn't sense a new dream surfacing or an old dream that had been pushed aside. I felt content and a bit uninspired.

Then the word *writing* came to mind.

What?! Where did that come from? Nope, that is not from the Lord. I'm not a writer; we've already established this. I chalked it up to random thoughts and quickly dismissed it.

At the conference that evening, I was asked to give a testimony about my leadership journey and owning my voice. I shared vulnerably and authentically, with humor woven through my narrative. Afterward, the editor of *The Well*, an online forum for women in the academy and professions, affirmed how much she enjoyed my testimony. And then came her next question: "Do you write?"

Ugh! Really, God? All of a sudden I felt like Jonah with this writing gig. I couldn't get away from it, and the Lord kept bringing it back around. I responded, "I'm not a writer, but I guess I'm going to learn how."

I had a choice in that moment. I could have said, "No, I don't write, thank you for asking." However, it was hard for me to ignore the multiple noes I'd given in this area, and God continued to bring it back around. Why was God giving me repeated chances to say yes? I wondered what I would miss out on if I continued to say no.

In the months that followed, I took a leap of faith, and Marcia, the editor, gave me constructive feedback and loads of encouragement in my writing. I learned much about the art and craft of writing from her and in working on the articles she posted. I also noticed something come alive in the hidden creative space of my soul. The more I pressed in to wrapping metaphors and words around my life experiences, the more Christ spoke truth into the lessons I learned. As I reflected on the truths the Spirit prompted me to write about, I felt an increased intimacy with God as well. I literally felt him writing with me.

As it often happens, life got busy, and once again, I shelved this yes to writing. It wasn't intentional. It just sort of happened. I didn't have time to keep up with it, especially with a new marriage and new projects at work. Achieving measurable goals at work and checking items off my to-do list at home seemed easier and pleased a lot of people too. People were blessed by my efficiency and productivity.

Writing, I discovered, was the antithesis of efficiency. It took time and patience. Writing had unpredictable moments of easy flow and writer's block. Creating something out of nothing required imagination and vision, which called for extra dependence on the Holy Spirit. This dependence is especially true for people like me who haven't tapped into this creative muscle for a while.

For the next couple of years, contentment in my efficient comfort zone led me to a passive no to creativity.

Until a phone call from Cindy Bunch, associate publisher at InterVarsity Press, interrupted my no. We talked about a project I led at work, when she subtly asked me a question, "Have you ever considered writing a book?"

"I really don't think I could pull that off. I don't think I have time, and I can't imagine what I could offer that hasn't been already said by someone else."

There, that should put an end to that conversation. But it didn't.

God continued to pursue me through the encouragement of Cindy and others. I wrestled with God and felt clenched fists and open hands to varying degrees as I mulled over this idea. The seed of writing did not want to go away, no matter how hard I tried. I knew I had a passion for making a difference in people's lives and did this naturally in relationships. Perhaps God wanted me to leverage the written word in this next season of life.

A year and a half later, I submitted a book proposal, inspired by God and cheered on by others.

Why did I hang on to my no for so long?

I think there is something unique in why we choose no in these creative spaces. There are many reasons why I did, and for me, I believe fear played a starring role. It felt increasingly risky and vulnerable to flex this creative muscle for the world to see. The more I wrote, the more I tapped into the deep well of my heart. This space felt sacred. What if people rejected my writing . . . or worse yet, rejected me? I could easily fail at this, which would then lead to all sorts of embarrassment.

In hindsight, encouragement from others, small steps in writing, my experiences in ministry, and my use of communication skills all worked together to help unclench my fists. As I became open handed, God revealed more to me about what to create and how we would do this together.

Even now, in the midst of writing this book, I still wrestle with doubt and fear. Impostor syndrome is real: *people will certainly find out I don't know what I'm doing.* I am learning to choose yes instead of no. There is freedom to have my identity anchored in Christ and not the opinions of others. There is a sense of fulfillment in seeing creativity as an act of worship instead of as an end product.

These creative parts of the soul may very well be the on ramps to greater worship and a bigger impact on the kingdom of God. Writing, music, art, gardening, and cooking are several examples of using our creative energy. We may think even more widely, to include any type of dreaming and crafting that brings a new idea to life: starting something from nothing, planting a new small group, opening a new business, or launching a new initiative a work.

If there were no obstacles, what creative space would you enjoy saying yes to?

We were meant to create, as God is our Creator. When this is stifled, it seems other things are suffocated as well: innovative ideas, thoughtful wisdom, and connection to Christ . . . just to name a few. What might you miss out on if you continue to say no to these parts of your soul? Furthermore, what might the world miss out on if you hang on to that no too much longer?

SPIRITUAL EXPERIMENT

To create a life map, begin by brainstorming memories from different stages of life. They might be milestones, but many can be ordinary events that shaped you as a person.

Reflect on transitions in life, moments that brought joy, events that were frustrating, and times you felt broken.

You may also want to include events or stories from your parents and grandparents. This information helps you to see how God has been at work even before your birth and can bring greater clarity to your own story.

Then put all of this into a timeline in order to see the flow of events. Sit with God and ask him to reveal some key observations about your story.

Share your life map with your small group or a trusted friend. Ask for their insight into your life map too. Pray that you may continue to be aware of God's sovereign hand on your life and open to his direction.

Chapter Ten

. . . .

SAYING YES, AGAIN

Yes is not a destination. It is a doorway to more adventures.

To be open to yes with God takes discipline, faith, and surrender. Once we've launched into the invitation with God, we may think we've finally arrived. We've accomplished the goal set before us. *Nicely done* we may think to ourselves.

Yet here is the thing about God: he always has more for us to experience. We limit him, and ourselves, with our small vision for our lives. If we are open, he will continue to work in and through us until we leave this earth.

I remember the activity books that occupied me for hours as a kid. Connect-the-dots puzzles were a favorite of mine. As I followed and drew lines between the scattered dots in numerical order, a picture came into focus.

Sometimes we say yes, and it's as if we connected dot number one and dot number two and then put the pencil down. We are satisfied with the segment we drew between these first two dots, as that took some initiative and courage. We don't realize there are many more yeses to be connected, which will create a beautiful

Sometimes when we say yes, we don't realize there are many more yeses to be connected.

picture in God's kingdom and our own souls. What could life be like if we were open to the big and small yeses, having the courage to say yes again and again and again? Might our yeses be connected individually and collectively for a greater purpose? I wonder what picture we could create connecting one yes to another yes, taking one dot at a time.

PRACTICING YES

Toni had practice saying yes over the years. She worked a decade in her company, received an MBA at Notre Dame, mentored up-and-coming leaders, and accepted multiple promotions. When she had the opportunity to consider a job in England, being open to possibilities was familiar territory. Toni and her husband entered into this decision process prayerfully and thoughtfully. Not only did they have Toni's career to consider, they also needed to think of her husband's vocation and the life of their three-year-old daughter. They had the choice to say no too. In fact, a few years prior, they did say no to a possibility overseas due to job fit and life stage.

Toni and her husband sought the Lord individually, together, and with the help of their spiritual community. They decided to take a leap of faith and say yes to England for the next several years. The opportunity would surely open more doors for Toni in her career.

As Toni packed for England, she connected dot one and dot two, and God prepared a host of other dots across the pond.

Toni flourished in this new role, and within eighteen months she said yes to a promotion that made her the first American woman under the age of thirty-five to manage this particular line in the organization. She centered her leadership on the integrity and character of Christ, which allowed her to care for and develop her staff with great intention. She also wrestled with her own insecurities as she led her team. God grew her character in the midst of leading. Toni reflected, "There are times I wish I could have had a redo because I would've done things differently— mainly been more vulnerable, not acted like I had it all together. There was some ugly mixed in with the good."

As Toni grew in her skills as a leader, she grew in her care for people she led. She discerned when to push for goals and when to stop and listen. Toni encouraged her team to bring their individual strengths to the table. She invited younger leaders to say yes to greater leadership in their department. She also grew in making space to care for people's hearts in the midst of everyday tasks. In particular, Toni remembers caring for a hurting employee who walked through a gut-wrenching divorce. She cultivated trust in the midst of work and life. People responded with gratitude, even saying she was one of the best bosses they'd had. Toni's yes to England not only grew the company's bottom line; it helped grow her team and her own leadership too.

This would be enough of an accomplishment. It takes a lot of work to adjust to new colleagues and a new culture, so looking for more yeses may seem a bit overzealous. It's not that Toni was looking for more to do; she only wanted to be open to God's movement in all areas of her life. After fifteen years of doing life with Jesus, she knew the more she sought his Spirit, the more fulfilled she would be. Where the Lord moved, Toni wanted to be a part of it.

God was at work in her nuclear family too. As they said yes to living in England, they experienced displacement in being a foreigner and learned what it felt like to be on the outside looking in. It was lonely and difficult at times, yet God expanded their relationships and worldview. They received radical hospitality from some new friends in England, and in turn, they wanted to give that warmth and welcome to others too.

Toni looked to her neighborhood and asked God to open her eyes to those who needed his love. She noticed there were several teenage girls living around her, and as she prayed, she felt led to invest in them. Toni's own life was impacted by others investing in her at a young age. Perhaps God would give her the opportunity to bless others in the same way. She befriended these young women, built trust, and eventually became a safe place to discuss the challenges in their lives. Eventually spiritual conversations evolved as Toni suggested Jesus would have something to say about these real-life issues. A Bible study developed, and one young woman surrendered her life to Christ! God connected a few more dots with this yes.

And then there was church. It was challenging for Toni's family to consider involvement with a community when they knew it would be for a limited amount of time. Toni wondered, *Is it even worth it?*

They decided yes, it was worth it, even if it would be for a few short years. Perhaps God could use their limited yes in an abundant way.

Toni's husband said yes to helping to lead the programming and teaching of kids' church every other Sunday. Toni commented that her husband "was the only man who faithfully taught kids' ministry. I have no doubt that his servant leadership and the way he offered a male perspective in that room will have a significant eternal impact on the lives of many kids in this church."

Toni decided to use her strength of hospitality by greeting everyone who came through the church doors with a smile. Albeit simple and small, this was what Toni could give in this season of life. Surprisingly, Toni thoroughly enjoyed serving in this way, and it seemed like others enjoyed her too.

In fact, several years later, after her family moved back to the States, they visited the church in England on a Sunday morning. As they started worship service the pastor paused and said, "If you haven't seen her yet, let's give a warm welcome to Toni who is visiting with us today. You may remember her as the woman in the red T-shirt, who smiled and said hello every Sunday morning!" The sanctuary erupted in cheers as they showed their appreciation and love. Who knew that a yes to hello and a smile would have such an effect? More dots connected with another small yes.

Toni's adventure to England advanced her career as she anticipated it would. She learned much about leadership and enjoyed achieving the goals set before her. In God's sovereignty and intricacy, he had more to offer Toni as she opened her eyes and heart to the people around her—yeses to heal, transform, and connect.

SURRENDERED TO YES

When I think of a life surrendered to the yes with God, the apostle Paul quickly rises to the top of the list. He took risks, said yes regardless of circumstances, and found tremendous joy in his yes. He seemed to always find a yes with God.

Willing to take risks. Before he started teaching and preaching about Jesus, Paul killed Christians. Being a Pharisee and enjoying the power and success that came with this role, he did not take kindly to Jesus disrupting their systems. Paul thought he needed to protect Jewish culture and guard against the false teachings of Jesus. He believed this so-called Messiah had caused nothing but chaos, and his followers had to be destroyed.

If this vengeful, self-righteous, Pharisee who murdered Christians could say yes to Jesus, I'm pretty sure anyone can. Maybe that's why God chose someone like Paul to do so much kingdom work. And not only did Paul say yes to Jesus once, he said yes repeatedly and led a life of yes with Christ.

Paul dove into the deep end and began taking crazy risks for the kingdom. From the beginning of his conversion to Christ, he started boldly preaching the news of Jesus (Acts 9). The same zeal that fueled his persecution of the church was now energizing his mission for Christ.

Acts 9:20-21 states:

> Immediately he began preaching about Jesus in the synagogues, saying, "He is indeed the Son of God!"
>
> All who heard him were amazed. "Isn't this the same man who caused such devastation among Jesus' followers in Jerusalem?" they asked. "And didn't he come here to arrest them and take them in chains to the leading priests?"

I can't imagine the shock people must have felt as they heard Paul preach. Likely there were folks who didn't trust him. I'm certain he experienced rejection and maybe even retaliation for the horrible things he had done. Christ compelled him to take the risks. Paul's identity was so anchored in Christ, it didn't matter if he failed or people rejected him. He knew he was secure in Christ. Paul allowed Jesus to direct his life.

Paul took his newfound faith and skill of preaching on the road. God had given him a vision for helping the Gentiles (people not of Jewish descent) know Jesus. This vision, fueled by the Lord, led him to cities all over Asia and Europe, with countless people surrendering their lives to Christ. This could not have been easy for Paul. He'd previously spent his life as a Pharisee in Jerusalem's synagogue. Now he took risks in foreign lands, finding anyone who would be open to learning about Jesus.

Paul planned one trip in particular to Asia and prepared to preach the good news of Jesus. However, the Spirit redirected Paul and his companions several times on their journey until they reached the province of Macedonia (modern-day Europe) and the city of Philippi. I'm not sure how Paul handled going from plan A, to plan B, then to plan C, but I would have struggled. Paul, though, trusted God's direction and took a risk to trust his plans and not theirs.

As Paul and his companions finally entered Philippi, they found Lydia, a successful businesswoman who gathered with a group of God-fearing women near a river for prayer on the Sabbath (Acts 16). They were spiritually seeking Gentiles, doing the best they could with the little information they had. When Paul shared the news of Jesus and the kingdom of God with these women, they received it and were baptized.

Paul took a risk and equipped these women, likely all part of Lydia's household. They formed the first European house church in her home. In Jewish culture, it was highly unusual for a Jewish man to interact with any woman, let alone a Gentile woman. Additionally, for Paul to equip these women to lead ministry must have seemed ridiculous in his Jewish tradition. Even if Paul was aware of Macedonian culture and the prominence women had in their culture, it still might have been a risk. He crossed cultural barriers and continued to walk through the doors God gave him. The church spread beyond Lydia's home as they said yes to spread this good news.

Paul moved on to share the gospel with more cities. He wrote his letter to the Philippians to encourage this new church in their yes as they followed Christ.

A yes in any circumstance. If you ever wonder where Paul wrote the books of the New Testament from, prison is typically a good guess. It was not because of crimes he committed but because he proclaimed Christ. Powerful people in the culture did not take kindly to Paul's message of Jesus as King. The Roman government declared Nero as "lord and king," not Jesus. If the people refused to worship Nero, into the prison they went. Paul wrote this letter to the Philippians while he was in a Roman prison. He encouraged the Philippians to imitate him and continue to say yes, despite the obstacles they would face.

This ongoing journey of yes would not be easy. What would sustain the Philippians and motivate them to persevere in following Jesus, especially with their mentor Paul in jail?

Paul reveals the secret to a faithful journey of yes in chapters three and four of his letter. He "learned the secret of living in every situation, whether it is with a full stomach or empty, with plenty or little" (Philippians 4:12). He learned how to be content with whatever he had. The outcome of the yes did not determine his belief in Christ.

In challenging circumstances, what would help you to be open to a yes?

Paul's unwavering faith in Jesus rooted him in all seasons and in all yeses. Paul wanted to know Christ in every way. In the good times and in the hard times, he wanted Christ. In chapter three, Paul encourages the Philippians to know Jesus not only in the resurrection but in his sufferings as well. In all situations, Jesus is present and has something to offer us. He will redeem. He will comfort. He will love. He will celebrate. He will be there. And he is enough.

Paul wasn't perfect, and he knew it. He continually understood his need for a Savior. In Philippians 3, Paul recounts all the ways he used to put his confidence in his pedigree, religious resume, and social status. Before he encountered Jesus, he was quite accomplished as a high-ranking Pharisee in Jerusalem. Paul had the equivalent of a Harvard degree, wealthy family, and lucrative job on Wall Street. But he didn't have Christ. Paul writes:

I once thought these things were valuable, but now I consider them worthless because of what Christ has done. Yes, everything else is worthless when compared with the infinite value of knowing Christ Jesus my Lord. For his sake I have discarded everything else, counting it all as garbage, so that I could gain Christ and become one with him. (Philippians 3:7-9)

This is not suggesting that saying yes to well-paying jobs and higher education is wrong. Paul is saying that once we experience saying yes to Christ and living a life open to him, we can't go back. It's worth exponentially more than any degree, job, or circumstance. Jesus is better . . . actually, Jesus is best, and Paul wouldn't have it any other way.

Finding joy in the yes. Paul's joy came from knowing Christ deeply and living into the purposes Christ had for his life. It seems that Paul could find something to be grateful for in whatever the yes produced because he knew the Lord was always at work and ever present, even if he couldn't see it.

It is intriguing that the word *rejoice* or *joy* is mentioned sixteen times in the book of Philippians. This is not a fluffy kind of happiness. It is a meaty, earthy joy. A joy that wells up from the grit of life and is secure in the hope found in Christ, not our circumstances. I suspect we can't know this joy unless we've experienced the pain. Philippians 3:1 says, "Whatever happens, my dear brothers and sisters, rejoice in the Lord. I never get tired of telling you these things, and I do it to safeguard your faith." A sustained faith is dependent on rejoicing in the Lord.

Jesus centered the yes for Paul. This foundation gave Paul vision, freedom, and joy as he continually said yes to live a life surrendered to Christ—a life lived purposefully, using his gifts to help bring hope and healing through Christ to the world.

THE COURAGE TO SAY YES, AGAIN

"Are you open to meeting someone new?"

Oh, the question I loved to hate. I'd been the victim of matchmaking and setups for over twenty years. I loved it, in that I met some really interesting people. I hated it because I usually felt horrible if it didn't work out. And it never worked out.

But because I was nearing the fourth decade of my life and still felt God asking me to be open to him in the realm of dating, I decided to go for it.

"Sure. Why not?!"

"Great, I'll pass along your contact information and let him reach out to you."

From my past experiences, I knew the chances of this random man contacting me were pretty slim. Many times the friend's motivation to see someone dating exceeded the desire of the one being matched.

I went about my fulfilling life, enjoying the season God had me in. The calendar said Thanksgiving, and gratitude swept over my whole life. I finished another round of counseling and read Ann Voskamp's book, *A Thousand Gifts: A Dare to Live Fully Right Where You Are*. Instead of focusing on the life I didn't have as I neared forty, I set my mind on choosing joy through gratitude . . . every day. Especially as I entered yet another holiday season, I could feel my heart ache for a family of my own. I doubled down on my time with Jesus and was on the lookout for God's gifts in my life.

I embraced Thanksgiving with my parents and enjoyed precious moments with them. Mom's delicious food packed with flavor and tender loving care. A 4:30 a.m. Black Friday run to Sam's Club with Dad, all in an effort to get that perfect TV for my apartment. Putting up the Christmas tree at my parents' home and reminiscing over every ornament. There's always a good laugh about the dilapidated Christmas bell made of tinfoil and pipe cleaner. I never was good with crafts.

What gifts of gratitude can you look out for today?

My heart filled with joy, and yet a longing ache lingered in the background. I packed up my car and drove back home. Then, I noticed a voice mail on my phone.

"Hello Christine. Kurt Wagoner here. David gave me your name. I wanted to see if you'd like to grab coffee sometime. Give me a call back when you can."

Stunned would accurately describe my feelings. It had been a long time since a man picked up an actual telephone, dialed, and left a voicemail. In an age of technology, it is easy to use texts and email, which are convenient enough but not as personal. He sounded nice and took surprising initiative, which I loved. A quick scan on the internet, courtesy of girlfriends I had called (I was driving, and this demanded immediate attention!) revealed that he was handsome, employed, and we had more mutual friends. This looked promising!

We met for coffee, and conversation rapidly evolved from background basics to passions in life, family dynamics, and spiritual journeys. Before I knew it, two hours had passed and I hadn't sipped my latte. This guy was for real. He pulled out the calendar on his phone and asked, "So when is the next time I could see you?" He spoke my love language with his high communication skills, planning, and initiative. We scheduled our next date for sushi, hugged goodbye, and I felt my heart race.

I couldn't decide if I was elated or having a panic attack.

I'd prayed to meet a man with similar values, a genuine heart, and good character. But I had been here before. I had said yes to dating men who seemed like a good fit. Then months, and sometimes years later, heartbreak ensued.

It seemed like a double bind. I desired to say yes and get to know Kurt. Simultaneously, fear gripped my heart, and I wanted to protect myself from any potential hurt. This season of gratitude proved to be a sweet time for Jesus and me. Would this ruin it or add to the joy?

I'm thankful for older spiritual friends in my life, who pat me on the back and give me a kick in the backside, all at the same time. I often need to get out of my head and hear truth from others that is rooted in God's Word and a loving heart. I remember one piece of advice my friend Linda gave me, "Bring your whole self to the table, Christine. Just be you. And whatever happens, you can trust in the Lord."

My immediate thought was, *Okay. As soon as I figure out who Christine is, I'll do that!*

Little did I know that this journey to say yes to date Kurt would uncover more of my true self. God knew long before I did that Kurt would bring out my strengths and that he would appreciate the gifts God had given me. I would learn what it means to have a true partnership.

But one thing became increasingly clear as I ventured into this new yes in familiar territory: my courage to say yes would need to be grounded in a trust of Jesus, not a trust in Kurt. Yes, to a certain extent I needed to understand if Kurt was trustworthy, and that would reveal itself over time. But my faith ultimately needed to be in God, not Kurt. One way to keep this in front of me would be to continue with my spirit of gratitude.

Remembering God's faithfulness to me became a spiritual discipline. Thanking him for the big and small ways he'd provided and cared for me over the years was a good place to start. Humans tend to have amnesia with God. We forget his mercies in our life and what he has done. The Lord must have known we would have this problem because the word *remember* is written repeatedly in Scripture.

As God often does, he put Kurt and me together to help bring healing to us and glory to him. Kurt had experienced his own set of heartaches in past relationships too.

Let's face it, the older you get the more disappointments you've weathered.

Individually and together, we said yes countless times in smaller ways as we built our relationship. Each time, God grew our confidence a little bit more. Yes to meeting each other's friends. Yes to interacting with family. Yes to spending more time together. Yes to holding pain for one another. Yes to forgiving and loving still. Finally, yes to a life spent together in marriage. That yes was accompanied by my high-decibel screams of joy, a massive snowstorm, and a big box of chocolates.

Living a life faithful to God and open to his invitations is never dull. While the big yeses have obvious impact, it's practicing yes in the ordinary days of life that holds significance. I've learned a lot from my neighbor Janie in this. When my husband and I moved into the neighborhood, she invited us over for peach pie on her back porch. Her ordinary yes to extend hospitality became meaningful as we instantly felt welcomed and seen. Janie would spontaneously text me and ask if I wanted to walk with her and another neighbor. Her ordinary yes didn't require extensive planning, but it did involve thoughtfulness. She invited me along with what she was doing that day and intentionally connected me with more neighbors. Janie could have gone on her usual walk with her established friends, which was predictable and comfortable. Instead, she took risks to include me, the new neighbor, and helped me feel more at home in this new place.

Janie enjoys serving others. When she discovered I needed to strip wallpaper in my kitchen, she offered her help. Taking wallpaper down might be one of the worst jobs in the world, and Janie said yes to rolling up her sleeves to tackle this project. I didn't ask her to help as I felt awful subjecting anyone else to this task. Instead, Janie rang my doorbell one day and had her calendar in hand saying, "We need to get this wallpaper project on the schedule. When can I come over and help you?" What made this ordinary yes even more profound was that Janie also had on her calendar surgery for the breast cancer she currently battled.

What small yes in your everyday life might extend God's kindness to someone?

I tried to block Janie's yes by saying she had too much on her plate, she didn't need to help me, and I couldn't possibly agree to her offer. Janie held up her hand and said, "I don't want to hear it. I'm helping you. You need this wallpaper to come down, and it might be a perfect distraction for me too."

Janie's ordinary yes blessed both of us. We not only stripped wallpaper, we shared more of our life stories, talked about our faith traditions, and laughed quite a bit. I prayed for Janie's surgery, which was the next day, and I grew even more grateful to God for giving me a neighbor like her.

We never know how God will use the ordinary to become extraordinary. There may be a yes buried in that no of yours, and it's just waiting to be set free. It may be waiting to ignite a new business, feed a hungry soul, or bring joy to a neighbor.

It's certainly a mystery in how a yes unfolds, and we can't predict what God will do. We can know with great certainty, though, that God's presence will go with us, and we will deepen our understanding and heart in him. May we be open to all that God desires to do through us and in us as we find our yes together.

SPIRITUAL EXPERIMENT

Practice gratitude. For a week, take a few minutes each day to note what you are thankful for. Pay particular attention to small things that happen in the day. Create a list on sticky notes in a visible place in your home in order to remind yourself of God's goodness and faithfulness.

ACKNOWLEDGMENTS

Finding my yes to write this book took time, encouragement, and much faith. I am blessed to have many people in my life who cheered me on as I ventured into this project.

My family is a constant encouragement. I continue to be overwhelmed with gratitude for the gift of my husband, Kurt. I'm thankful for his support, prayers, and love for me as I spent hours alone writing. I'm grateful for my parents who instilled confidence and love in me as a child and continue to do so in my life. Dad, we need to create another five-year plan. And thank you to all the siblings, in-laws, and extended family who have prayed and sent much love over the last few years of this project.

I'm thankful for InterVarsity Press and the countless people who bring life to a book and support the author while doing it. Many thanks to Andy Le Peau for recognizing my ability to write before I did. Much gratitude to my editors, Ed Gilbreath and Cindy Bunch. Ed, thank you for your input and guidance, which made this book stronger. Cindy, I'm glad you asked if I had a book in me and am grateful for your wisdom and encouragement as I navigated saying yes to this project. A special thank you to all those involved with the InterVarsity Staff Publishing

Consultation, hosted at IVP. This key event cast vision for writing, gave practical advice, and provided space to hear from God. And much gratitude to all those behind the scenes in marketing, contracts, copyediting, public relations, cover artists, and many more who made this book, and every book, beautiful and accessible to readers.

My heart overflows with love for my writing group, who met monthly as I wrote my first draft. Cara, Tracy, Rebecca, and Dana, your edits, constructive feedback, and positive comments for each chapter created a much better book than I ever could have written on my own. You all have made me a better writer. Thank you for cheering me on to the finish line and praying with me when I wasn't sure I'd make it.

My gratitude to all who entrusted me to tell their stories of yes in this book. Thank you for sharing God's work in your lives and the lessons you learned in the yeses. I'm in awe of your faith in Christ and am inspired to be all the more open to God's invitations in my life.

Many thanks to the InterVarsity colleagues and students who I've had the privilege of ministering, leading, and growing alongside of for the last twenty-two years. Special thanks to my late IV mentor, JoAnne Fields, who helped me grow in my call to ministry and in my character simultaneously. My life is forever changed as a result.

Finally, I'm indebted to our Lord Jesus Christ for giving me words and creativity when I had none. For giving me courage when I doubted. And for the many holy moments of reflection while writing. He made this book come to life and may he receive the glory and honor.

DISCUSSION GUIDE

CHAPTERS 1-3

1. When have you said no or felt hesitant about an opportunity? How open were you to the possibility of saying yes?

Read Luke 19:11-26.

2. What do you observe about the King, the servants, and the people listening to Jesus?

3. Why do you think the first two servants chose to invest their silver?

4. What "silver" might God be inviting you to invest?

5. What do you believe about God's desire to see you experience joy as you invest this "silver"?

6. What may have caused the third servant to bury his silver?

7. What prevents you from being open to yes? Is there an obstacle mentioned in chapters 1-3 that resonates with you? Explain.

8. How might you advocate for someone's yes by uncovering a blind spot they hold? Or one you may hold?

9. In the parable, the King's rewards and consequences reveal his priorities. How are God's values reflected as well?

10. What would you need from God to take a next step toward a yes?

Debrief Spiritual Experiments

- What did you enjoy about the experiments?
- What did you find challenging about the experiments?
- What is God revealing to you?

CHAPTERS 4-5

1. Have you ever said yes to something that seemed unusual to others? What was it and why did you say yes?

Read Judges 4.

2. What do you notice about Deborah's character and leadership?

3. What were Deborah's smaller steps of yes that led her to the battlefield in verse 14?

4. How might Deborah have experienced resistance from others in her yes?

5. What can we learn from Deborah and Barak's partnership?

6. How could you encourage someone to be open to an invitation God has for them?

7. If you invited someone to join in your yes, how could that multiply the impact of the yes? Who might that person or people be?

8. How could you create space to debrief a recent yes to one of God's invitations?

9. In what ways has your relationship with Christ grown because of this yes?

Debrief Spiritual Experiments

- What did you enjoy about the experiments?
- What did you find challenging about the experiments?
- What is God revealing to you?

CHAPTERS 6-8

1. When has a yes been painful in your life? What questions did it cause you to ask?

Read John 19.

2. In verses 1-16, what do you observe about Pilate, the Jewish leaders, and Jesus?

3. What are the power dynamics in this scene and how does Jesus respond? What does this reveal about Jesus?

4. Reread verses 17-37. Imagine you are a person in the crowd watching Jesus' crucifixion. What strikes you in this scene?

5. Why would Jesus choose to endure such a painful death?

6. Reread verses 38-42. What kinds of questions might Jesus' followers be asking at this point?

7. The crucifixion happened on Friday and the resurrection occurred on Sunday. John Ortberg calls that Saturday the "in-between day," noting that it's a time "between despair and joy" and "between confusion and clarity." How do you respond to waiting for God's fulfillment of a yes when the future is uncertain?

8. What helps you trust God in these difficult times? What do you need from God to help you trust him more?

9. Jerry Bridges said we should "preach the gospel to yourself every day." What aspect of the gospel do you need to be reminded of today? How will this make a difference in the way you live or how you think?

Debrief Spiritual Experiments

* What did you enjoy about the experiments?

* What did you find challenging about the experiments?

* What is God revealing to you?

CHAPTERS 9-10

1. Consider your current circumstances. What might be good reasons to consider a no instead of a yes? How might you discern this with the Lord?

2. Have you ever said no to an opportunity in order to enable someone else to say yes? What motivated you to make this choice?

Read Philippians 3.

3. What do we learn about Paul's sources of confidence?

4. What gives you confidence to continue being open to God's invitations?

5. What do you observe about the role of joy and gratitude in Paul's life?

6. How might joy and gratitude be involved in your yes?

7. Why is Paul motivated to continue saying yes to Christ? Why do you continue to say yes to him?

8. The small invitations God gives us often have great impact, especially as we regularly notice them. What small yes might extend God's kindness to someone else?

9. How is God shaping you as you practice living a life open to yes?

Debrief Spiritual Experiments

- What did you enjoy about the experiments?

- What did you find challenging about the experiments?

- What is God revealing to you?

NOTES

1 YES OFTEN STARTS WITH NO

7 *one mina equaled:* Note to Luke 19:13, Holy Bible, New International Version®, NIV® Copyright ©1973, 1978, 1984, 2011 by Biblica, Inc.

2 SHIFTING OUR PERSPECTIVE

24 *hidden biases:* "Q&A with the Authors of Blindspot," accessed October 8, 2020, http://blindspot.fas.harvard.edu/FAQ.

25 *everyone holds hidden biases:* "Unconscious Bias," University of California, San Francisco, Office of Diversity and Outreach, accessed November 7, 2020, https://diversity.ucsf.edu/resources/unconscious-bias.

3 DISCOVERING INTERNAL RESISTENCE

36 *world record for balls juggled:* "Most Balls Juggled," *Guinness World Records,* accessed November 7, 2020, www.guinnessworldrecords.com/world-records/most-balls-juggled.

37 *Middle Eastern value of hospitality:* Chani, Noah, "Hospitality in the Arab World," Arab America, July 10, 2019, www.arabamerica.com/hospitality-in-the-arab-world.

39 *women were a rejected group:* E. Earle Ellis, *The Gospel of Luke,* New Century Bible Commentary (Grand Rapids, MI: Eerdmans, 1974), 162.

4 STARTING SMALL

58 *seventy percent of Rwandan pastors:* "History," ALARM, African Leadership and Reconciliation Ministries, accessed November 7, 2020, www.alarm-inc.org/history.

59 *spiritual gifts assessment:* Here's a free online assessment: "Welcome to the Spiritual Gifts Survey," Team Ministry, accessed November 7, 2020, https://gifts.churchgrowth.org/spiritual-gifts-survey.

5 GROWING THROUGH YOUR YES

64 *Deborah is the first woman:* Michael Wilcock, *The Message of Judges,* The Bible Speaks Today (Downers Grove, IL: InterVarsity Press, 1992), 59.

66 *Deborah encouraging humility:* Wilcock, *Judges,* 62-64.

71 *Discipleship Cycle:* "Discipleship Cycle," Twentyonehundred Productions, August 27, 2013, https://2100.intervarsity.org/resources/disciple ship-cycle.

72 *Life moves pretty fast: Ferris Bueller's Day Off,* directed by John Hughes (Hollywood, CA: Paramount Pictures, 1986).

6 YES ... BUT

89 *A polyp grew:* I wrote on this topic previously: Christine Wagoner, "Re-Imagining Motherhood," *The Well* (blog), InterVarsity, May 5, 2014, https://thewell.intervarsity.org/blog/re-imagining-motherhood.

7 WAS YES A MISTAKE?

97 *the Jews despised King Herod:* Rodney A Whitacre, "The Glory Is Revealed Among the Despised: A Herodian," *Mark,* The IVP New Testament Commentary Series (Downers Grove, IL: InterVarsity Press, 2010) www.biblegateway.com/resources/ivp-nt/Glory-Is-Revealed -Among-Despised-640.

99 *he likely spent the night somewhere:* Bruce Milne, *The Message of John* (Downers Grove, IL: InterVarsity Press, 1993), 91.

8 THE PAIN OF YES

118 *preach the gospel:* Jerry Bridges, *The Discipline of Grace* (Colorado Springs, CO: NavPress, 2006), 59-60.

9 THE CHOICE TO SAY NO

126 *Sarah Breuel quote:* "Speaker, Sarah Breuel," Urbana 18 General Session, St. Louis, MO, December 31, 2018, https://urbana.org/message/sarah-breuel.

10 SAYING YES, AGAIN

143 *a risk to equip women:* Gordon D. Fee, *Philippians,* IVP New Testament Commentary Series (Downers Grove, IL: InterVarsity Press, 1999), 26.

144 *if people refused to worship Nero:* Fee, *Philippians,* 30-31.

DISCUSSION GUIDE

157 *in-between day:* John Ortberg, *Who Is This Man? The Unpredictable Impact of the Inescapable* (Grand Rapids, MI: Zondervan, 2012), 175-76.

preach the gospel: Jerry Bridges, *The Discipline of Grace* (Colorado Springs, CO: NavPress, 2006), 59-60.